Problems of Philosophy

General Editor: D. J. O'CONNOR

Each volume in this series provides a short introductory study of one of the main problems of philosophy. An account is given of the ways in which the given problem has been seen in the history of philosophy, and of the principal solutions which philosophers have advanced.

An important feature of the series is that in each study the language and the treatment are as simple as is compatible with a serious presentation of the philosophical difficulties. A full bibliography is included.

MEMORY

Don Locke

MACMILLAN

© Don Locke 1971

First published in the United States 1971
First published in Great Britain 1971

Published by
THE MACMILLAN PRESS LTD
London and Basingstoke
Associated companies in New York Toronto
Dublin Melbourne Johannesburg and Madras

SBN 333 10159 6

Printed in Great Britain by
FLETCHER AND SON LTD
Norwich

Contents

MEMORY

1

The Representative Theory

Our first questions are obvious. What precisely is memory? What is it to remember something? These philosophical questions need to be distinguished from the similar questions that might be asked by a psychologist or neurologist. There are problems about how memory operates, about what goes on in our body or brain when we remember, about what physical and psychological factors help or hinder our remembering, and so on. These are the concern of the scientist, who investigates the functioning of the human capacity we call memory. But our question is different; we are asking what memory is in itself, what that human capacity consists in, however it may operate. We want to explain not the mechanism of memory, but its nature; not how it works, but what it is. The question is, in effect, what it is that we are talking about when we talk about memory, as we all do, without knowing anything of the physical processes involved. When we say that we remember something, what are we referring to? When we talk about remembering, what, exactly, are we talking about?

Now, if we consider what happens when we remember things, an obvious answer suggests itself. When I remember something, I recall it, or bring it back to mind. In a way, it is as if I were experiencing it again, although my present experience, the memory-experience, is very different from my original experience of what I now remember. On the one hand, I may be remembering it incorrectly; on the other hand, the way in which I am now aware of it is very different from the way in which I was aware of it at the time—memory experiences are vague, fleeting, altogether weaker and less vivid than straightforward perceptual experiences. Nevertheless, these experiences provide us with information about the past. It is because I remember these things that I know what happened, although if my memory plays me false I will be mistaken in thinking that such things did happen.

This natural and obvious account of what memory is has also been the most common since it was adopted almost universally among philosophers, from ancient Greece until the present day. It has, however, taken two different forms, which have been distinguished as the Representative theory and the Realist theory. We will begin with the former, for it has been by far the most widely held, by philosophers ranging from Aristotle to Bertrand Russell. This Representative theory can be summarized thus:

The Representative Theory

To remember is to undergo a certain sort of mental experience. In particular, it is to experience an image, a memory-image, which reproduces some past sense-experience. The image might even be said to be literally a reproduction of the original sense-impression, which has, in the meantime, been stored away in the mind. This image provides us with the information we are then said to remember; it is because we have and experience the image that we have the particular piece of memory-knowledge.

But, like so many philosophical theories, this account of memory answers some questions—what is memory? What mental processes or entities does it involve? How does it provide knowledge of the past?—only to raise others. The distinctive feature of the Representative theory, obviously enough, is that memory is held to involve representations in the form of memory-images of what has happened. But this raises difficulties.

One such difficulty stems from the fact that these representations, the memory-images, are things that occur now, when we are remembering, so that, according to the theory, what we apprehend when we remember is not what has happened, but what is happening now. But if that is so, how can memory be awareness of the past? So Aristotle wondered "how it is possible that, though perceiving only the impression, we remember the absent thing which we do not perceive" (*On*

3

Memory and Reminiscence, p. 609; for full details of all references, see bibliography). Aristotle's answer is that, just as we can see Coriscus when we look at a portrait, because the portrait is a representation of Coriscus, so we can be aware of the past when we have the present experience, because the present experience is a representation of the past. But the question now is, in what way is the present image a representation of what has happened? Or, as Aristotle puts it, "Why should the perception of the mere impression be memory of something else, instead of being related to this impression alone?"

One suggestion might be that this present image is not so much a fresh impression that represents the past event, as the original sense-impression produced all over again. Thus, John Locke, in the first edition of his *Essay Concerning Human Understanding*, had spoken of memory as "the storehouse of our ideas," in which the various experiences we have had are laid up out of sight until we revive them. Many other philosophers have made the same suggestion. St. Augustine, in particular, waxed lyrical about "the great harbour of memory, with its secret, numberless, and indefinable recesses," which takes in the things we experience "so that they may be reproduced and brought back again when the need arises. They all enter the memory by their various ways and are stored up in the memory. Or rather it is not the things themselves that enter; what happens is

4

that the images of things perceived are there ready at hand for thought to recall" (*Confessions,* Book X, chapter 8).

But this idea of memory as a storehouse seems on reflection little more than an attractive metaphor. For where are these ideas and experiences supposed to be when we are not examining them? How can an idea exist without our being aware of it? This difficulty leads Locke to add, in the second edition, "But our ideas being nothing but actual perceptions in the mind, which cease to be anything when there is no perception of them, this laying up of our ideas in the repository of memory, signifies no more but this, that the mind has a power, in many cases, to revive perceptions which it has once had, with this additional perception annexed to them—that it has had them before. And in this sense it is that our ideas are said to be in our memories, when indeed they are actually nowhere, but only there is an ability in the mind, when it will, to revive them again" (Book II, chapter X, section 3).

Yet even this will not do, as Thomas Reid points out: "But it seems to me as difficult to revive things which have ceased to be anything, as it is to lay them up in a repository, or to bring them out of it. When a thing is once annihilated, the same thing cannot be again produced, though another thing similar to it may. Locke acknowledges in another place that the same thing cannot have two beginnings of existence, and that things that have different beginnings are not the same but diverse. From this it follows that an ability to revive our ideas or perceptions, after they have ceased to be, can signify no more but an ability to create new ideas or perceptions similar to those we had before" (*Essays on the Intellectual Powers of Man*, p. 355). It is clear, then, that the Representative theorist has to regard the present memory-experience as quite separate from the original sense-experience, though the one is supposed to resemble the other.

The question now is how we are to tell that the present experience does reproduce or represent what was previously experienced. For we cannot define memory simply as having images, since we have images of many things we do not remember. Not all images are memory images; it is even possible for a completely accurate mental representation to be a product of mere imagination. So if memory is to be defined in terms of image reproductions, we need some way of distinguishing memory-images from pure imagination. This need is especially pressing if we want to base knowledge of the past on memory, for if we cannot tell whether a certain image comes from memory or from imagination, how can we possibly claim knowledge on account of it? In this way Representative theorists have been led to seek out, in their memory-experiences, some feature that stamps them as memory-experiences. This has been called the search for a "memory indicator," the element that shows that an image is a memory-image, does represent the past, and so provides knowledge of the past.

Probably the most famous discussion of this problem is that of David Hume. He suggests that the ideas of memory differ from those of imagination in two respects: "It is evident at first sight, that the ideas of the memory are much more lively and strong then those of the imagination, and that the former faculty paints its objects in more distinct colours than any which are employed by the latter. When we remember any past event, the idea of it flows in upon the mind in a forceful manner; whereas in the imagination the perception is faint and languid, and cannot without difficulty be preserved by the mind steady and uniform for any considerable time. Here then is a sensible difference betwixt one species of ideas and another. . . . There is another difference betwixt these two kinds of ideas, which is no less evident, namely that . . . the imagination is not restrained to the same order and form with the original impressions; while the memory is in a manner tied down in that respect, without any power of variation" (*Treatise of Human Nature,* Book I, part I, section III).

A bold attempt, but an obvious failure. For a start, I remember seeing my grandfather when I was young, but the idea I form of him is certainly not lively or strong or distinct; rather it is, as Hume says of the imagination, "faint and languid, and cannot without difficulty be preserved by the mind steady and uniform for any considerable time." On the other hand, I can form extremely vivid ideas of certain philosophers I have never met nor even seen a photograph of, though no doubt they are not at all as I imagine them to be. Indeed, paradoxically for Hume, the more distinct and vivid my idea of my grandfather becomes, the less I am inclined to regard it as memory and the more I am inclined to think I must be making it up. Nor is it true that when we remember things, as opposed to imagining them, we remember them in the order in which they were originally experienced. It may well be that in remembering last night's disastrous party, I remember first the arrival of the police, then the fight that led to their arrival, then the argument that led to the fight, and finally the drinks I drank that led to the disagreement in the first place.

A second celebrated attempt to distinguish memory from imagination is that of Russell in *The Analysis of Mind*. Russell here suggests that memory images are distinguished from other images by two feelings that accompany them: "feelings of familiarity," which lead us to trust the images, and "feelings of pastness," which lead us to refer them to some time in the past. This theory is difficult to assess because Russell tells us very little about the nature of these feelings. It might seem, for example, that the "feeling of familiarity" itself involves memory and so cannot be used to explain it, although Russell does say that "the judgement that what is familiar has been experienced before is a product of reflection, and is no part of the feeling of familiarity" (p. 169). There is also the possible objection that if I imagine a scene often enough, that image will become more familiar than many memory images, and that if I imagine something for a second time, that image may well carry with it some "feeling of pastness." But quite apart from these difficulties, it is once again clear that this theory will not do, that the sense of familiarity and the sense of pastness are not sufficient to establish that the thing in question is remembered. People often think they are remembering when in fact they are only imagining; the mere fact that what they imagine seems familiar and seems past does not insure that it did happen and so does not establish that this is memory rather than imagination.

There have been other attempts to distinguish memory from imagination (e.g., R. F. Harrod, "Memory," p. 51; Brian Smith, *Memory*, pp. 140–45), but it should be clear by now that nothing is going to provide the desired intrinsic feature that shows that a memory-experience is a memory-experience. So long as it is possible for people to be mistaken, or even unsure, about whether they are remembering, as opposed to imagining, then it seems it cannot be anything about the experience itself that tells us which it is. What makes an image a memory-image is not some feature of the image, but the fact that it represents some past event that we have experienced, and there is no way in which we can tell that from the image itself. Indeed, the Representative theory seems to have it exactly the wrong way around; it suggests that we establish from the experience itself that we are remembering, and so conclude that what we remember did happen; but in fact we have to refer to what happened in order to tell whether or not we are remembering.

How, then, did Hume, Russell, and others come to make this mistake of looking for the distinction between memory and imagination in the memory-experience itself, when it lies rather in the relationship between the experience and what has actually happened in the past? One answer is that the Representative theorist has to look for the distinction within the experience because, according to him, it is only by memory that we can find out what has actually happened; we cannot begin by ascertaining past events and then use them to establish that we have a case of memory, because we have to use memory in order to ascertain past events! A second answer, following on from this dilemma, is that Hume and Russell may be concerned not so much with the question of what distinguishes memory from imagination, as with the question of what leads us, rightly or wrongly, to regard a particular experience as memory rather than imagination. For the fact is that we do claim to remember various things without stopping to check the present experience against the past facts, and if we are in doubt, considerations of vividness, familiarity, and so on may well be relevant. We certainly say things like "But it must have happened—I can see it so clearly, even now."

Thus, when Hume later comes back to this problem of the difference between memory and imagination, he rejects his second suggestion, that it lies in the order of the ideas, saying, ". . . though it be a peculiar property of the memory to preserve the original order and position of its ideas, while the imagination transposes and changes them as it pleases; yet this difference is not sufficient to distinguish them in their operation, or make us know the one from the other; it being impossible to recall the past impressions, in order to compare them with our present ideas, and see whether their arrangement be exactly similar" (*Treatise*, Book I, part 3, section 5). What distinguishes memory from imagination is its relationship to "past impressions," but this cannot be how we tell them apart, since it is impossible to recall those past impressions. How, then, do we tell whether we are remembering or imagining? By the force and vivacity of the images involved, says Hume. The point comes out more clearly in Russell, when he writes, "Our confidence or lack of confidence in the accuracy of the memory image must, in fundamental cases, be based upon a characteristic of the image itself, since we cannot evoke the past bodily and compare it with the

11

present image. . . . I think the characteristic by which we distinguish the images we trust is the feeling of *familiarity* that accompanies them" (*Analysis of Mind*, p. 161). Once again, the question is not what constitutes memory as opposed to imagination, but what leads us to think we are remembering rather than imagining. And Russell's answer is the familiarity of our images.

J. O. Urmson suggests that the point is that there are two possible distinctions between memory and imagination. We can distinguish between what a person correctly remembers (= memory) and what he thinks he remembers but does not (= imagination); and we can also distinguish between what a person, rightly or wrongly, thinks he remembers (= memory) and what he deliberately invents for himself (= imagination). That is, by "memory" we might refer to successful, accurate remembering as opposed to unsuccessful, inaccurate remembering; or we might refer to the attempt to remember, whether successful or unsuccessful, as opposed to free invention. When we are remembering in the second sense, we might be imagining in the first sense, i.e., we might set out to remember something but get it wrong; and when we are imagining in the second sense, we might be remembering in the first, i.e., we might think we are making it up when in fact it is something that we remember.

Now, whether we have memory or imagination, in terms of the first distinction, depends on the relationship between the present experience and what has happened in the past; but so far as the second distinction is concerned, the distinction between trying to remember and simply making it up, ". . . it is immediately obvious that I do know, immediately, which I am doing, without collecting evidence about my life history, for I need no evidence. . . . Evidence is unnecessary because I know straight off whether I am, say, daydreaming or story-telling on the one hand or recollecting (well or ill) on the other" (J. O. Urmson, "Memory and Imagination," p. 86). This suggests that there must be some special feature of the experience of remembering, as opposed to imagining, in this second sense, which enables us to tell, straight off and without evidence, which it is; the puzzle is only that although everyone can make the distinction, we find philosophers disagreeing about what that special distinguishing mark is. The explanation, as Urmson suggests, is that the difference lies not in some special feature of the experience, but in what we are trying to do, in our intentions, our criteria of success and failure. Suppose we are remembering or imagining ourselves conducting the defense in a trial. To tell which it is, "we do not have to look for any special feature of our mental pictures or the tale we tell, nor need we ascertain their relationship to reality or anything else. All we have to do is know which criteria of success are applicable, and that is a question which depends upon our own intentions.

We are recollecting not if we did conduct the defense in the trial, but if it matters whether we did. We are imagining if some such criteria of success as general verisimilitude, or interestingness, are the relevant ones" (pp. 87–88).

Indeed, R. F. Holland has argued that with this particular distinction between memory and imagination it is logically impossible that we should think we are remembering when in fact we are imagining, or vice versa, so we have no need of any special "memory indicator" to distinguish the two. "The idea that one could do this ('feign some past scene of adventure') and at the same time think one was remembering, were it not for the special character of the ideas involved, seems to result, in part at least, from the misconstruction of a logical impossibility as a kind of psychological impossibility. Small wonder that the Memory-Indicator, the allegedly distinctive experience which is supposed to distinguish memory from imagination, should appear to be at once unmistakable and indescribable" ("The Empiricist Theory of Memory," p. 471). If this is right, then Hume and Russell are equally mistaken in trying to find the difference between remembering and imagining in the experience itself, whichever of the two distinctions they are concerned with.

However, I think there is a further factor to be taken into account. We sometimes find ourselves, to use a neutral expression, thinking of a face or a place or an incident without being sure whether this is something we are remembering or something we have imagined in Urmson's sense of "freely invent." This is often true of scenes we are tempted to locate in our early childhood, if only we could be sure they really happened. Now, in such a case we cannot decide whether it is memory or imagination by referring to our intentions, because here we do not deliberately produce the thoughts and images; rather, they occur to us. It seems to me that both Urmson and Holland overestimate the extent to which imagery in memory and imagination is voluntary and deliberate. Holland, for example, concentrates on the case in which one is asked to remember something, and says, "One cannot, as Hume thought, contemplate an idea of the memory and an idea of the imagination and, feigning ignorance of their origins, begin to distinguish them afresh by means of a difference in their respective qualities" (p. 486). True enough, but there are also cases in which one finds oneself with an image without knowing whether its origin is memory or imagination. It is in this sort of case that Hume's and Russell's criteria operate. But on the other hand, if Urmson and Holland overestimate the extent to which imagery is voluntary and deliberate, it is even more obvious that Hume and Russell underestimate it. Normally we do not have to discover whether we are remembering, in this sense of trying to recall, or whether we are imagining, in this sense of making it up, because normally "we tell just by knowing what we are at, knowing whether we have or have not chosen to act so that resemblance to actuality is a criterion of the success of our activity" (Urmson, p. 90).

It seems, then, that Hume and Russell were correct in thinking we can know, without reference to the past, whether we are remembering, trying to recall, as opposed to freely inventing, though mistaken in thinking we always tell this from some special feature of the experience involved. But when we turn back to the other possible distinction between memory and imagination, that between remembering correctly and mistakenly thinking we remember, then we cannot tell one from the other without reference to the past. Certainly, we can tell immediately—or rather we can know without having to tell—that an image is meant to be a memory-image, but we cannot tell from the experience alone that the image does represent something that has happened and which we experienced. This means not only that we cannot tell whether the image is genuinely a representation of previous experience, but also that we cannot rely on the image to provide us with knowledge. To establish that the image does represent what happened, that it is correct and so can be used to provide knowledge, we have first to establish what happened and then check the present image against it. But how can we do that if, as the theory insists, remembering is simply a matter of having the image? To discover whether it is a correct memory-image, we have to get outside the image and ascertain what happened, but the only way of ascertaining what happened is via the image. The Representative theorist finds himself imprisoned within his imagery, with no way of confirming that the imagery does reveal the past, as it has to if we are to have memory-knowledge.

Thus Thomas Reid found the same difficulty in the Representative theory of memory that others have found in the Representative theory of perception. The Representative theory of perception is that what we are aware of when, as we put it, we perceive things, are not the tables and chairs, trees and rivers, in the world around us, but "ideas," which are produced in our minds by those external things. Similarly, the Representative theory of memory is that what we are aware of, when we remember, are not the events, places, and people we experienced in the past, but images of those past things, which are produced in our minds. The difficulty for both theories is that in restricting what I am aware of to these ideas or representations in my mind, they equally restrict what I can know of to these mental entities. If all I am aware of are the representations, the "ideas" or images, how can I know that there are external things at all, much less that these external things are the causes of my present ideas? In this way, the Representative theory of perception effectively undercuts itself and, Reid argues, precisely the same happens to the Representative theory of memory.

"It may be observed, that the common system,

that ideas are the only immediate objects of thought, leads to scepticism with regard to memory, as well as with regard to objects of sense. . . . Ideas are said to be things internal and present, which have no existence but during the moment they are in the mind. The objects of sense are things external, which have a continued existence. When it is maintained that all we immediately perceive is only ideas of phantasms, how can we, from the existence of those phantasms, conclude the existence of an external world corresponding to them? . . . The same difficulty with regard to memory naturally arises from the system of ideas; and the only reason why it was not observed by philosophers is, because they give less attention to memory than to the senses; for, since ideas are things present, how can we, from our having a certain idea presently in our mind, conclude that an event really happened ten or twenty years ago, corresponding to it? There is the same need of arguments to prove, that the ideas of memory are pictures of things that really did happen, as that the ideas of sense are pictures of external objects which now exist. In both cases, it will be impossible to find any argument that has real weight. So that this hypothesis leads us to absolute scepticism, with regard to those things which we most distinctly remember, no less than with regard to the external objects of sense" (*Essays on the Intellectual Powers of Man,* pp. 357–58).

18

Thus the Representative theorist effectively cuts himself off from the only way we have of telling whether a particular experience is a genuine memory-experience. It is hardly surprising, therefore, that Hume and Russell turn aside to the separate problem of what makes us think we are remembering rather than imagining. For if we are ever to know that the image is a genuine memory-image and does correctly represent the past, then we will need some other form of remembering to tell us that it does so. In fact, Reid shows that Locke and Hume both implicitly assume some other, *non*-representative form of memory in order to explain our memory representations. Locke, for example, says that in memory the mind revives "perceptions which it has once had, with this additional perception annexed to them—that it has had them before." But Reid says, "Whether we perceive them to be the same, or only like to those we had before, this perception, one would think, supposes a remembrance of those we had before, otherwise the similitude or identity could not be perceived" (p. 355). Again, when Hume says that "we find by experience that, when any impression has been present with the mind, it again makes its appearance there as an idea," Reid wishes "to know what we are here to understand by experience? It is said, we find all this by experience; and I conceive nothing can be meant by this experience but memory—not that memory which our author defines, but memory in the common acceptation of the word. According to vulgar apprehension, memory is an immediate knowledge of something past. Our author does not admit that there is any such knowledge in the human mind. He maintains that memory is nothing but a present idea or impression. But in defining what he takes memory to be, he takes for granted that kind of memory which he rejects" (p. 357; a similar point is made by G. E. Moore, *Some Main Problems*, pp. 245–47).

It seems, then, that the Representative theory suffers from two crippling disabilities. The theory is that to remember is to have an image that represents some past event or reproduces some past experience. But if the image is all I have to go on, I can never tell whether it does do this, and so cannot know whether it is a memory image at all—though, as Urmson points out, there is no difficulty in establishing that that is what it is meant to be. So the Representative theory makes it impossible for us to know whether we actually are remembering, as opposed to trying to remember or thinking we remember; and as a consequence of this, it makes it impossible for memory to provide us with knowledge of the past or of anything else. If we are to avoid these difficulties it seems that, as Reid argues, we will have to make use of some other form of remembering, a form in which memory is, in Reid's words, "an immediate knowledge of something past," rather than the awareness of some present representation.

2

The Realist Theory

The Realist theory of memory hopes to avoid the
difficulties inherent in the Representative theory
by maintaining that what we are aware of, when
we remember, are not representations of past
items, but those past items themselves—just as,
according to the Realist theory of perception,
what we are aware of, when we perceive, are
not ideas or representations of objects in the
world around us, but those objects themselves. As J. Laird puts it, "Memory does not
mean the existence of present representations of
past things. It is the mind's awareness of past
things themselves" (*Study in Realism*, p. 56). This
Realist theory has been by no means so wide-
spread as the Representative account, but it was
common in the first quarter of this century, presumably through the influence of Henri Bergson,
for whose metaphysics the notion of "pure memory," a direct awareness of the past, was of central
importance. Other notable Realists were Alexander, Stout, and Laird, and more recently
Woozley, Earle, Taylor, and Smith; the theory
was also held, in a rather different form, by

Moore, Russell, and Price (for references, see below and bibliography).

The Realist theory derives most of its plausibility from our very conception of memory. As Reid said, it is one of the "things obvious and certain with regard to memory [that the] object of memory, or thing remembered, must be something that is past" (pp. 339–40); yet the Representative theory seems to be suggesting that what we remember is something present, an image. Russell warns us, "There is some danger of confusion as to the nature of memory, owing to the fact that memory of an object is apt to be accompanied by an image of the object, and yet the image cannot be what constitutes memory. This is easily seen by merely noticing that the image is in the present, whereas what is remembered is known to be in the past" (*Problems of Philosophy*, pp. 114–15). Certainly the Representative theorist cannot plausibly maintain that the present image is what we remember; rather he will say, following Aristotle, that although the image is what we are aware of, what we remember is what the image represents. But even this sounds paradoxical: what we are aware of when we remember is not what we remember! This is precisely what the Realist denies; he insists that, when we remember, we are aware of the past thing itself.

Notice, however, that this does not commit the Realist to denying the role of mental imagery in remembering; to do that, would be to suggest that memory is not to be construed by analogy with perception at all. Rather, the Realist will say that what we call the memory-image is not a present existent at all, but is the past event or experience itself as it appears to us in our remembering. G. H. Stout points out, "In remembering a past experience, I do not, normally, discriminate the memory-image from the experience remembered" ("In What Way Is Memory-Knowledge Immediate?" p. 160), and it can be argued on independent grounds that it is a mistake to think of memory-images as present entities that exist at a time quite different from what they are images of. A. D. Woozley makes the point clearly: "What seems peculiar to memory is not the materials of it, but the cognitive relation involved; and the image is not a *thing* at all distinct numerically from the thing remembered. . . . What the word 'image' stands for here is a certain mode of awareness, the way an object appears when it enters into a memory situation (or imagination situation). Because in remembering we are trying to recall the original event as it was at the time of its occurring, we are led to distinguish between it as it looked then and it as it looks now; while such a distinction is natural and valid enough, we have no ground whatever for going to make the further distinction of treating the original as one *thing* and the present memory-image as another *thing*. If we see that there is no case for this latter distinction, we find that many of the traditional puzzles over memory disappear, namely all the puzzles of dualism generated by the supposed imitative relation holding between a memory-image and its original; if we start by inventing *things* of a peculiar sort, which do not in fact exist, and by calling them images, we are bound to store up insoluble puzzles for ourselves; but if we realise that images are not things at all, different from their originals, then the puzzles which depended on their being things disappear" (*Theory of Knowledge,* pp. 64–65).

So the Realist theory of memory can be taken as the theory that to have a memory-image is to be aware, in a unique and characteristic way, of past events. What we call the image is no more than the way this past event appears to us when we so remember it. Remembering is compared not with looking at pictures, but with looking at things themselves (see R. Taylor, "The 'Justification' of Memories and the Analogy of Vision"). This, presumably, is what S. Alexander is getting at when he writes, cryptically, "The pastness of the object is a datum of experience, directly apprehended. The object is compresent with me *as* past. The act of remembering is the process whereby this object becomes attached to or appropriated by myself" (*Space, Time and Deity,* pp. 113–14).

As might be expected, the standard objections to this theory of memory are precisely analogous to the standard objections to the Realist theory of perception. Thus, for example, C. D. Broad (*Mind and Its Place in Nature*, pp. 257–61; see also E. J. Furlong, "Memory and the Argument from Illusion") points out that the memory-image may differ in many respects from the item remembered, which suggests that the image cannot exactly be what is remembered. The answer to this is that when we describe the memory-image, we describe the item as we remember it, as it appears to us in our remembering, and this may very well differ from what actually was the case. It is now sufficiently well understood that the fact that a thing appears different from what it really is does not mean that we cannot be perceiving that thing itself; this applies equally whether we are talking about perception or about memory. A second objection of Broad's (pp. 252–56) is that the one thing may be remembered at different times, which suggests that, according to the Realist, images occurring at numerically different times are nevertheless one and the same thing. The answer to this is that, if we are prepared to talk about numerically distinct appearances—which is what memory-images amount to on a Realist view—at all, there is no reason why we should not be aware of numerically distinct appearances of one and the same thing at different points in time, just as we may be aware of numerically distinct appearances of one and the same thing from different points in space.

The more serious objection to the Realist theory is that it remains totally unexplained how in memory we can be aware of the past, of what no longer exists. Aristotle says, "One might as well suppose it possible also to see or hear that which is not present" ("On Memory and Reminiscence," p. 610). And when Reid writes, "It is by memory that we have an immediate knowledge of things past," his editor, Hamilton, adds the tart footnote, "An *immediate* knowledge of a past thing is a contradiction. For we can only know a thing immediately, if we know it in itself, or as existing; but what is past cannot be known in itself, for it is non-existent" (*Essays on the Intellectual Powers of Man,* p. 339). Commenting on this in turn, Laird insists that the past does exist, although, of course, it does not exist *now;* existence includes past existence, and there is therefore no difficulty about direct acquaintance with the past (*Study in Realism,* chapter III). Or as Price puts it, talk of a past event being present to consciousness need not mean that that past event exists again in the present; it may mean only that it is presented to us and that we are now aware of it: "Nothing prevents a past event from being presented to consciousness, though it may be a contradiction to say that a past event could be present in the sense of 'now existing'" ("Memory-Knowledge," pp. 25–26). But none of this brings me personally any nearer to understanding how this strange quasi-perceptual awareness of the past operates.

Moreover, it is not at all clear that the Realist theory in its present form avoids the objections to the Representative theory. It may—or may not—be an advantage to speak of a mysterious form of awareness of the past rather than of a form of awareness of mysterious present entities, but the major difficulties remain. We saw that the Representative theorist seems to have no way of telling from the experience whether or not he is genuinely remembering, and therefore cannot use memory in order to arrive at knowledge of the past. The problem remains, irrespective of whether we think of the experience as looking at some present representation or whether we think of it as looking at an appearance of the past event itself. This may seem surprising, since we arrived at the Realist theory precisely in order to avoid that problem. It has been argued, for example, that since we can check the accuracy of our memory-images, we must have a direct awareness of the past to check the images against. Thus Russell claims, "We are certainly able to some extent to compare our image with the object remembered, so that we often know, within somewhat wide limits, how far our image is accurate; but this would be impossible, unless the object, as opposed to the image, were in some way before the mind" (*Problems of Philosophy,* p. 115); and H. H. Price, "Memory-images are often inadequate and known to be so. If we can detect their inadequacy and correct it, surely we must have some 'direct acquaintance' with past events themselves" (*Thinking and Experience,* p. 309). G. E.

27

Moore, in a discussion that is so characteristically painstaking as to be beyond both quotation and parody, comes to a similar conclusion in *Some Main Problems* (pp. 237–47).

However, the Realism here suggested by Russell, Price, and Moore must be different from the Realism considered so far, for they are arguing that we must have a direct awareness of the past *independent* of our awareness of the memory-image. Russell goes on, "Thus the essence of memory is not constituted by the image, but by having immediately before the mind an object which is recognized as past." The difficulty now is to explain how the past object can be "immediately before the mind" when all we seem to be aware of is the image; and when Moore insists that in memory we are conscious of the past event itself in a way that differs from our consciousness of the memory-image, he is totally unable to explain what this consciousness of the past event amounts to: "All that can be said, I think, with certainty, is that you are conscious of it, in the obscure sense in which it is necessary that you should be conscious of it, in order to know that it was different from the image. . . . This obscure sort of consciousness is what I said that even those who admit its existence seem unable to give a clear account of. And I confess I can't give any clear account of it myself. I can only try to point out what it is, by pointing out that it is what occurs in this instance" (*Some Main Problems*, p. 246).

The Realist Theory

The solution to these difficulties is that memory is not to be thought of as a form of consciousness or awareness at all, but as a form of knowledge. Almost alone among those who adopted the Realist approach, Stout explicitly distinguished the claim that memory provides an immediate experience of the past from the claim that it provides immediate knowledge of the past (see "In What Way Is Memory-Knowledge Immediate?" though he is less clear in his later *Mind and Matter*). Stout suggests that to say that memory directly acquaints us with the past is not to say that it provides some inexplicable immediate awareness or experience of things that no longer exist, but that it provides us with immediate knowledge of the past; where by "immediate knowledge" he means non-inferential knowledge, such that the ground of the memory judgment "is not capable of being known by itself in such a way as to be asserted in a proposition distinct from the memory judgement itself as premiss is distinct from conclusion" (p. 179). That is, Stout is suggesting that, when I make a memory judgment, this judgment is not based on some present experience of remembering, but is simply a report of what I know about the past, and as such is not based on anything apart from the fact that I know it.

Now this approach to the problem completely undercuts the traditional theories of memory, since it amounts to denying that remembering is an experience that informs us of the past. Rather, remembering is itself a form of knowledge of the past, which may operate independently of any present experience whatsoever. There are, then, two quite distinct theories, both of which might be called Realist theories. One is that in memory we are aware of past events, so that what we call a memory-image is in fact the past event as we experience it, as it appears to us in our remembering. The other is that memory provides a form of knowledge of the past that is immediate and direct in the sense that it does not depend on a present experience at all, whether that experience is thought of as an awareness of a present representation or an awareness of a past item. I am going to restrict the label "Realist theory" to the first of these, since that is the view in which memory is construed in analogy with perception. But it is this view that suffers from the same difficulties as the Representative theory; it is only the second view that takes account of the fact that we can often know that the past event was not like the image we now have of it.

At the beginning of this chapter I said that the Realist theory was common only toward the beginning of this century, and I think it no accident that it led quickly to a view of memory that replaces both it and the Representative account. For if memory is explained as direct awareness of the past, this "direct awareness" might refer either to some form of experience of past events, in which case we have the Realist theory proper, or it might refer to Stout's non-inferential knowledge of the past. Indeed, the two interpretations will hardly be distinguished as long as it is held, as in Russell's theory of knowledge by acquaintance, that the only way of knowing something directly or immediately is to experience it. But once we distinguish knowing from experiencing, the way is open for an entirely different approach to the problems of memory, according to which remembering is not a type of experience, but a type of knowledge. To this contemporary approach we can now turn.

3

The Contemporary Approach

If we go back to the "obvious" account of memory sketched at the very beginning of chapter 1, we can see that it incorporates three basic claims, all of them central to both the Representative and the Realist theories:

1) Remembering is an occurrence, something that happens, more particularly something we do;

2) This occurrence consists in a mental experience, involving the having of mental images, whatever they may be;

3) It is because we have these experiences, these memory-images, that we know various facts "from memory," i.e., memory-knowledge is knowledge based on or derived from the memory-experience or memory-image.

In the recent discussion of the topic, these three central claims have all been questioned and virtually abandoned. Certainly, we must examine them more closely than we have so far.

First of all, when I sketched that original theory of memory I wrote, "Now, if we consider what happens when we remember things . . . ," but it might well be said that this starts the whole discussion off on the wrong foot, since there are times when we talk about remembering, when we say that someone remembers something, when nothing is happening, when that person is not doing anything at all, at least not anything that could be called remembering. We might, for example, say of a man who is sound asleep or absorbed in a book, that he remembers the result of every British election in this century, and this is not to say anything about what is now happening or what he is now doing.

How serious an objection is this? It is clear that sometimes, as in this example, the word "remember" is not used to report an occurrence—let us call that a "non-occurrent use." But it is equally clear that sometimes the word is used to report an occurrence, as when I say, "Good Heavens, I've just remembered I left the gas on"—let us call that an "occurrent use." Now, it might well be argued that the non-occurrent uses of "remember" are parasitic on the occurrent uses, in that to say that a man remembers something, even when he is not actually doing anything that might be called remembering, is to refer indirectly to cases in which he is doing something called remembering, or to report an ability or disposition to remember in the occurrent sense. Thus, to say of the man who is sound asleep or absorbed in a book, that he remembers the election results, might be to say that he can remember them and on occasion does remember them. In just the same way we can say of a man who is sound asleep or silently absorbed in a book, that he speaks fluent French, and although we are not referring to anything he is doing at the time, this does not show that speaking is not an occurrence—something that happens or something we do. Rather, to say that he speaks fluent French is to say that he can do it and on occasion does do it.

The suggestion is, then, that the non-occurrent use of "remember" depends on the occurrent use. But is this so? Although there are acts or occurrences of remembering, as in our example of my suddenly remembering I left the gas on, it does not seem that all cases of remembering involve such acts or occurrences. I remember where I have parked my car, even though I do not think about its position from the moment I leave it to the moment I get back to it. Or take the man who remembers the election results: Does he do anything we would describe as an act of remembering? Certainly, he reels off the results, and answers snap questions correctly, but are these acts or occurrences of remembering in the way that uttering a sentence is an act or occurrence of speaking? I think we apply the occurrent use of "remember" only where something is remembered in thought, where the remembered thing is brought or comes to mind; we talk about an occurrence of remembering that I left the gas on, because this thought suddenly strikes me. We would not, in the same way, describe saying out loud, "The gas is on," or the election expert's answers to our questions, as acts of remembering. As Shoemaker says, "There is no use of the word 'remember' in which a person who has answered a question correctly and without effort, thereby showing that he remembers . . . something in the nonoccurrent sense, can be said to have been remembering that thing while answering the question, and to have ceased remembering it as soon as he has finished answering the question and turned his mind to other matters" ("Memory," p. 271). It may also be significant that we do not naturally use a present continuous tense, "is remembering." Certainly we would hardly say, as our expert reels off the results, "He is now remembering the results," as we would say of a man making a speech in French, "He is now speaking fluent French."

But although we speak of an act or occurrence of remembering only where the remembering consists in thinking something, silently and internally, there are nevertheless various things we do—listing results, answering questions, etc.—that count or qualify as remembering in the way that nodding your head counts as agreeing with what is said. Listing the results may not be what we mean by "remembering," any more than nodding your head is what we mean by "agreeing," but if someone lists the results we will say, "He remembered the results," just as if someone nods his head, we will say "He agreed with us." Similarly, walking directly back to my car, and not having to stop and look for it, counts as remembering where I parked it, even though walking straight up to it can hardly be called "an act of remembering." So the truth seems to be not that remembering always involves acts or occurrences of remembering, but that it involves various acts or occurrences that count or qualify as remembering, in the way that going straight back to my car counts as remembering where I parked it.

This is an important conclusion, for what counts as remembering will differ from case to case. What counts as remembering where my car is parked is not at all like what counts as remembering the election results. Indeed, quite different things can count as remembering the one thing; I might walk directly back to my car, I might tell someone else where to find it, or I might draw a map—these are all different activities, but they all qualify as remembering where the car is. So, at the very least, we have to modify the first claim of the traditional theories of memory to read not "Remembering is something that happens, something we do," but rather "Remembering is a matter of what happens, of what we do." But that is not all, for the traditional theories are also based on the assumption that, in all cases of remembering, there is some common thing that we do, that all cases of remembering have in common a particular mental experience. This now seems to be a mistake. The argument so far forces us not only to modify the first claim of the traditional theories, but also to question the second.

These theories maintain that the occurrence common to all cases of remembering is some form of mental occurrence, typically thought of as the having of a mental image. Now it is undeniable that often when we remember things we do have images, but it is also undeniable that often we do not. The man who remembers the election results may have what is sometimes called a photographic memory; he may repeat the results by "reading them off" from a vivid image of a table in a history book, which he can recall at will. But he may not; it may be that he has learned the list by heart, so that he can run through the results without having any imagery whatsoever. This dispensability of imagery is particularly obvious when we consider our remembering particular facts. I can remember that Brutus stabbed Caesar without forming any images of that murder, and there are some facts I remember, where I do not know what images to form; I remember that $E = mc^2$, but I cannot imagine what an appropriate image of that fact would be. Even where we do have imagery when we remember, the images often seem to function as mere illustrations, rather than being the act of remembering. While I try to remember Nelson's dying words, I may form an image of him lying on the deck of the *Victory,* but this image is hardly the remembering; it is more like the illustration in a storybook. (For further discussion of the role of imagery in memory, see A. J. Ayer, *The Problem of Knowledge*, pp. 134–42; B. S. Benjamin, "Remembering.")

The third main claim of the traditional theories is that memory provides us with knowledge, in the sense that we know various facts about the past because of the memory-experiences we have. But once we question the role of these memory-experiences in remembering, we are also going to question whether memory-knowledge is knowledge based on such experiences. When, for example, I remember that Brutus stabbed Caesar or that $E = mc^2$, there do not seem to be any special memory-experiences that inform me of these facts. When I say that I remember that Brutus stabbed Caesar, I am not saying that I know this because of some special experience I now have; I seem to be saying no more than that I know it. What, after all, is the difference between remembering some fact and knowing it? Surely, in a majority of cases, "remember" and "know" are interchangeable. The only difference seems to be that if I remember some fact I must have learned it in the past, whereas if I know something because of what I now observe, that cannot count as remembering. And since most of our knowledge is knowledge we have acquired in the past, most of our knowledge is memory-knowledge, and "know" is

38

usually replaceable by "remember." The traditional theories view memory as a source of knowledge, but the truth seems rather to be that memory is already a type of knowledge; to remember that kumaras are sweet potatoes is precisely to know that they are, so my remembering that kumaras are sweet potatoes cannot be what gives me this knowledge, cannot be the source of the knowledge.

It turns out, then, that all three central claims of the traditional theories are mistaken. Stout was right to suggest that memory consists not in immediate experience of the past, but in immediate knowledge of the past; memory is to be thought of not as a form of quasi-perceptual awareness, but as a form of knowledge. Certainly, this has come to be the standard contemporary account of the nature of memory; to remember something is to know it, where this knowledge has been acquired in the past. As Ryle puts it, remembering "is like going over something, not getting to something; it is like recounting, not like researching" (*Concept of Mind*, p. 275); "it is akin not to learning lessons, but to reciting them" (p. 276). But one problem remains; if the traditional theories are as mistaken as all that, how did they come to be adopted at all, let alone come to be the dominating theories through centuries of philosophical thought? The explanation is obvious enough: In thinking of memory as a matter of reproducing or re-experiencing past events the traditional theorists were clearly thinking of the special case of remembering events from one's own past. Certainly, philosophers have always concentrated on this particular type of memory, and some have even gone so far as to deny that we can ever remember anything except what we have experienced for ourselves. Thus, for example, Von Leyden states, "Everyone would agree that what we can remember is not just any past event or fact, but a certain kind of past event or fact, namely those that form part of one's own previous experience" (*Remembering*, p. 60). This is an astonishing suggestion. It means, for example, that I cannot remember anything about ancient history, since ancient history does not form part of my own previous experience. Clearly, my school-teachers must have been wasting their time!

Even those philosophers who have realized that not all memory is restricted to this particular form of personal memory have tended to insist that personal memory is the most important and characteristic form of remembering. Bergson, and Russell following him, distinguished between what he called "habit memory," the rote memory of such facts as that Brutus stabbed Caesar, and "pure memory," the spontaneous recollection of particular happenings, and dismissed the former as a mere "motor mechanism." But whether or not Bergson was right in thinking "habit memory" unimportant, it is clear that any fully adequate theory of memory will have to take account of it, not least because most of our remembering seems to be of this sort. This, obviously, is what the traditional theories fail to do. In concentrating on one particular form of memory, they fail to provide a correct account of memory in general; there are more forms of memory than are dreamt of in their philosophies. Of course, one of the traditional theories might still be correct regarding the particular form of memory in which you remember something that once happened to you. But before we can decide on that, and so arrive at a final evaluation of these traditional theories, we should first say something about the various forms that memory can take.

4

The Forms of Memory

Many different philosophers have drawn many different distinctions between many different forms of memory. Broad even goes so far as to say, "The word 'memory' is highly ambiguous. . . . It is quite certain that the word covers a number of very different acts. We talk of remembering a set of nonsense syllables; of remembering a poem; of remembering a proposition in Euclid, though we have forgotten the words in which it was expressed when we originally learnt it; of remembering past events; and of remembering people, places and things" (*Mind and Its Place in Nature*, p. 221). But this does not show that the words "memory" and "remember" are ambiguous (see Benjamin, "Remembering," p. 318). The word "insult" also covers a wide range of acts—spoken words, drawings, gestures, actions—but that does not make the term ambiguous. Better to talk not of ambiguities or different senses of the word "remember," but of different kinds of remembering, different forms of memory.

Of the various distinctions that philosophers have made, the most important for our present purposes is Bergson's distinction, taken over in more or less modified form by Russell and by Ayer, between "habit memory" and "pure memory" (Russell calls the latter "true memory"; Ayer calls it "event memory"). This distinction is fundamental to Bergson's metaphysics: habit-memory is a mere motor mechanism, a function of the brain and nervous system, as when we recite some lesson we have learned by heart; but pure memory, the recollection of specific events, is a function of the mind or spirit, by means of which we are aware of the past, and which cannot consist in any purely physical or mechanical activity. However, the interest of the distinction for us is that, in making it, Bergson, Russell, and even Ayer hope to separate that particular form of memory, to which the traditional theories seem to apply, from other and perhaps less-important varieties. Certainly Bergson and Russell, respectively, interpret pure memory according to the Realist and Representative theories, and Russell insists, "It is this sort of occurrence that constitutes the essence of memory. Until we have analysed what happens in such a case as this, we have not succeeded in understanding memory" (*Analysis of Mind*, p. 167; for Malcolm's criticism of this claim, see p. 133 below).

Unfortunately, the distinction, even as modified by Ayer, is much too crude. Bergson and Russell have in mind the difference between remembering something that has been learned by

heart—hence the label "habit-memory"—and recollecting some specific item or incident. But many
cases of remembering do not fall into either cate-
gory, and some fall into both. Suppose that, after
a struggle, I manage to remember an argument
put forward by a certain philosopher, and I do
so, as well I might, without recalling any particular occasion on which I heard or read the argument. This is not a case of pure memory, but
neither is it a case of habit memory. As I labor
to recall the various things that philosophers have
said about memory, I will only be insulted to be
told that this is the mere functioning of a mechanical habit. I do not know these things by heart
in the way I remember my multiplication tables;
instead I have to put a lot of *thought* into it.
On the other hand, someone might make a habit
of recalling some particular occasion, so that
whenever anyone mentions the war, he immediately launches into the same old story of how he
crossed the Rhine. This would, presumably, be
both pure memory and habit-memory at once.

Bergson and Russell go wrong in thinking that
remembering must be either a matter of knowing
by heart (habit-memory) or a matter of recalling
in imagery (pure, or true, memory). Thus Russell is led to say, "Suppose you ask me what I ate
for breakfast this morning. Suppose, further, that
I have not thought about my breakfast in the
meantime, and that I did not, while I was eating
it, put into words what it consisted of. In this

case, my recollection will be true memory, not habit-memory. The process of remembering will consist of calling up images of my breakfast" (*Analysis of Mind,* p. 175). But this seems unlikely. I may very well remember that I had bacon and eggs without having to form any images of my breakfast, even if I have not thought about it in the meantime or otherwise committed the menu to heart. The likelihood is that Russell remembers what he had for breakfast in precisely the way he remembers how Caesar died, i.e., he knows the answer and gives it when asked. In either case, he may or may not have images, but they are irrelevant in that he can answer the question without having to refer to them. But because, like Bergson, he operates with the oversimple distinction between knowing by heart and recalling in imagery, Russell is forced to conclude that remembering your breakfast, not being the former, must be the latter.

There are difficulties even for Ayer's much more sophisticated distinction between habit-memory and event memory (*Problem of Knowledge,* pp. 134–42). The former, for Ayer, is remembering that consists in being able to do something, which includes not only cases where what is remembered is itself an ability, such as remembering how to swim or how to set a compass, but also cases where what is remembered is some matter of fact, like remembering that Brutus stabbed Caesar, where this remembering consists in being able to tell others that this happened. Event memory, on the other hand, is the recollection of particular occurrences that, Ayer insists, need not involve mental imagery. First of all, Ayer is perhaps too restrictive in speaking of "event" memory, for we can in the same way recollect particular people, places, and things. Nor is this equivalent to remembering some incident that involved those people, places, or things. I can, for example, recall the Cathedral Square of my home town quite vividly, without remembering any particular incident that occurred there or recalling any particular occasion on which I saw it. But a more important difficulty is that there are cases of remembering that do not consist in a general ability to do something, and yet are not cases of "event memory" either. Halfway to work I suddenly remember, with a shock, that today is Sunday; this is not the recollection of some particular item or incident from the past, but neither is it a case of habit-memory.

This last example suggests that Bergson, Russell, and Ayer are all in their different ways running together two quite different distinctions: one between remembering an item or event from the past, and other sorts of remembering, such as remembering a fact or how to do something; the other between remembering on some specific occasion, and the general ability to remember, i.e., between "remember" in what we called its occurrent use and "remember" in the non-occurrent use. In contrasting our general ability to remember various facts and skills with specific occurrences of remembering items and events from the past, they leave out of account the general ability to remember items and events from the past and specific occurrences of remembering facts and skills. So perhaps it will be clearer if we concentrate now not on the general ability to remember various things, which is where talk of "habit" might come in, but on different kinds of remembering, whether occurrent or non-occurrent.

We have seen that the contemporary approach is to regard memory as a form of knowledge, and there is a familiar distinction between three types of knowledge, or three different ways in which we speak of knowing things: we speak of knowing that something is the case, that it is so—we can call that "factual knowledge"; we speak of knowing how to do something, which amounts to possessing some skill or ability—we can call that "practical knowledge"; and we speak of knowing some particular person we have met or place we have been—we can call that "personal knowledge." Now it seems that we can make exactly the same distinctions between different types of remembering, since we also speak, in very much the same way, of remembering that something is the case, remembering how to do something, and remembering some specific person, place, thing, or incident. So let us distinguish between three forms of memory: factual memory, practical memory, and personal memory.

These three forms of memory, like the analogous forms of knowledge, are not entirely separate, and on occasion they overlap and interrelate. Remembering how to drive a car involves remembering that it starts by turning a key; remembering a place involves remembering various facts about that place; and so on. Again, remembering Hamlet's soliloquy might be classified as personal memory (remembering the speech) or as practical memory (remembering how to recite it) or as factual memory (remembering that the words are "To be or not to be . . ." etc.). And although the three forms are each associated with a particular grammatical construction —remembering *that* such-and-such, remembering *how* to do such-and-such, remembering *such-and-such itself*—grammar provides only a rough guide to which form of memory is involved. Remembering someone's name seems to be factual memory rather than personal memory, i.e., remembering that his name is Smith; remembering how my father speaks may be personal memory rather than practical memory; remembering a tune may be practical memory (remembering how to whistle it) or perhaps even factual memory (remembering that it goes da-da-di-dum-dum . . .) rather than personal memory; and so on.

There are also several other ways in which we talk about remembering, which may or may not indicate yet further forms of memory. Thus we speak of remembering where something is, when something happened, what something is, how something goes, and remembering to do something. Remembering what something is, for example, seems to be a case of factual memory, remembering that it is a certain thing or kind of thing, but it is not so obvious that remembering where something is is the same as remembering that it is in a certain place—I may be able to take you to it though I cannot describe where it is. Similarly, remembering to do something could be classified as factual memory, equivalent to remembering that something is to be done, but that something is to be done is not exactly a fact—it might rather be said to be a prescription. There are also other, more-specialized usages, such as "Remember me to your wife," "Remember, remember, the Fifth of November," or "I'll remember you in my will." Then there are other things connected with memory, such as being reminded of something or recognizing someone. Being reminded is not the same as remembering, for your voice may remind me of someone though I cannot remember who it is; nor is recognizing the same as remembering, for I might recognize someone I have never met before from a description, and that is not remembering him.

No doubt any complete and final philosophical

account of memory should include an exhaustive discussion of all these factors, and many others besides. But there is not the space for that here, even supposing that such an inquiry would be at all fruitful or interesting in the absence of any particular problems it might raise or solve. So I propose to concentrate on what seem to me the three most important and central forms of memory: factual memory, practical memory, and personal memory.

5
Factual Memory

Factual memory seems, most clearly of all, to be a form of knowledge; to remember that Brutus stabbed Caesar or that $E = mc^2$ is, in the main, to know these facts. More precisely, factual memory is factual knowledge that has been acquired in the past and does not come from present experience or observation. This is not to say, as some have thought, that factual memory is restricted to knowledge of the past. We can remember facts about the present and even about the future, as when I remember that today is Tuesday or that I have an important appointment in the morning. The distinguishing feature of factual memory is not that it is knowledge *of* the past, but that it is knowledge *acquired in* the past. I use "acquired" as a general term for the many and various ways in which we can come to know things. There are, for example, some facts we know that we can hardly be said to have learned. I may remember and so know that I had a bad toothache a month back, but I did not learn that fact, nor did anyone teach it to me.

However, factual memory cannot be defined

simply as knowledge acquired in the past, because there is always a lot of information we have acquired and forgotten. Rather, we should define factual memory as retained factual knowledge, i.e., as knowledge we have possessed before and still possess. This definition serves to rule out only such factual knowledge as is acquired at the time in question, as when I know that something happened because I now read about it in a book. Remembering a fact is incompatible with having just learned it; if you remember it, then you knew it before.

Now, it might be argued that factual memory cannot be defined in terms of factual knowledge, since we sometimes draw a distinction between the two. Certainly, we often say things like "I know his name but I just cannot remember it" or "You knew we were expecting visitors this evening; you should have remembered it," and this suggests that there must be some difference between remembering something and knowing it. One way around the difficulty would be to suggest that "know" and "remember" here refer to different times; I knew his name once, but at the moment I do not. But I think a better explanation lies in the distinction between the occurrent and non-occurrent uses of "remember." I do not remember the man's name in the occurrent sense, i.e., I cannot bring it to mind now, but I do remember it non-occurrently, as is shown by the fact that it comes back to me later; I cannot re-

member it now, but I have not lost the general
ability to remember it, and a single failure does
not show that I have lost the ability (cf. stalling
a car when you start it). So when we say, "I know
his name but I cannot remember it," this amounts
to "I (non-occurrently) remember his name but
I do not (occurrently) remember it." We prefer
the former form of words because "know" does
not naturally have an occurrent use in the way
that "remember" has, and this makes it convenient to state the point in terms of a distinction between knowing and remembering—even though
it could be said that at the time in question I do
not know the man's name any more than I remember it. Still, the example does not affect the
definition of non-occurrent factual remembering
in terms of knowledge; occurrent factual remembering, on the other hand, would have to be explained in terms of actualizing the knowledge,
bringing it to mind.

A second difficulty for the definition of factual
memory in terms of factual knowledge is suggested by Malcolm ("Three Lectures on Memory,"
pp. 223–24): A man sees a bird without knowing
what sort of bird it is, and then later discovers
from a book that such birds are cardinals. He says,
"I remember that I saw a cardinal last week," but
it is not true that he knew before now that it was
a cardinal; he has only just learned that it was.
Malcolm suggests that this is a case of what might
be called "impure" factual memory, involving an

53

elliptical use of the verb "remember"; what the man says amounts to "I *remember* that I saw a bird, and I *now know* that it was a cardinal." I think this same solution can be given for another of Malcolm's difficulties (pp. 239–40), the case of the man who suddenly remembers that he had a strange dream the night before, though he was not aware, at the time, that he was dreaming. We can explain "I remember having a dream" as amounting in the same way to "I remember having certain experiences, and I now know that it was a dream," though his idiosyncratic theory of dreaming prevents Malcolm himself from accepting this solution.

However, I am not sure that Malcolm's notion of an elliptical use of the word "remember" enables us to deal with another, more puzzling, case. Suppose someone asks me whether a certain student, whom we both want to see, was present at my lecture. When I lecture, I tend not to notice what is in front of me—my mind is on what I am saying, not what I am seeing—so it may be that during the lecture I did not consciously notice whether anyone was sitting in the back row. But now, when asked, I recall that the student was there, sitting in the back row, though I did not notice it at the time. If I had noticed him, I would have said something to him, but I did not; it is only now that I remember he was there. So here, once again, I remember something I had not previously known. And this time it will not help to say that I remember that someone was there and now know that it was he, because this "remember" simply repeats the difficulty. Even at the time, I did not know that anyone was there, though in some sense I must have noticed him, perhaps unconsciously, or else I could hardly recall him, as I now do. This seems a definite counterexample to our definition of factual memory, but later on (p. 100 below) I will suggest that it is not a case of factual memory, after all.

A further objection has been suggested by C. B. Martin and Max Deutscher ("Remembering," pp. 167–71). They argue that it is possible for a person to remember without realizing that he remembers; so far from knowing the facts in question, he may actually be convinced they are false. Suppose, to use an example of Malcolm's, that a man has what he regards as a recurring fantasy of having been kidnaped as a child, of having been seized by three masked men and driven off in a green car, etc.; and in fact all this did happen to him, though his parents have kept it secret from him. Here it is natural to say that he remembers being kidnaped, even though he does not know that it happened. As it stands, this is not an objection to the definition of factual memory in terms of factual knowledge, because the memory involved is memory of a certain incident, an instance of personal memory, rather than memory of a fact. Yet it may seem that, to the extent that we want to say the man remembers being kidnaped and put in a green car, etc., we will equally want to say that he remembers *that* he was kidnaped, that he was put in a green car, etc.

Malcolm himself allows that *if* we say he remembers the kidnaping, we should equally say that he remembers that he was kidnaped, but Malcolm thinks it is not clear that we should even say that he remembers the kidnaping: "There are opposing inclinations here, and I believe it is neither clearly right to say he remembers it nor clearly right to say that he does not" (p. 213). Even so, to the extent that it is right to say that the man remembers it, to that extent this will be an objection to the definition of factual memory in terms of factual knowledge. Other philosophers, however, have different inclinations from Malcolm. Stanley Munsat, for example, wants to say that the man remembers being kidnaped without saying that he remembers *that* he was kidnaped, etc. ("Does All Memory Imply Factual Memory?"). And so long as we say this, there is no difficulty for the definition of factual memory in terms of factual knowledge. My own inclination is to agree with Munsat.

So much for the difficulties about defining factual memory in terms of factual knowledge; there are further difficulties in defining factual memory as *retained* knowledge. To say that knowledge is retained is, presumably, to say that it has been acquired in the past and not forgotten in the meantime. But what is the relationship between the present knowledge and the past knowledge? The obvious suggestion is that the present knowledge depends on the past knowledge, and, accordingly Malcolm defines factual memory thus: "A person, B, remembers that p if and only if B knows that p because he knew that p" (p. 223). But what sort of dependence is this; what is the force of the "because"? Malcolm insists that it is not a causal dependence; the "because" is not a causal "because," but amounts rather to "If B had not known that p, he would not now know that p"—like the "because" in "He is called John because his uncle was called John," which amounts to "If his uncle had not been called John, he would not have been called John," but does not mean that his uncle's name caused his name. (This is my own example, rather than Malcolm's.)

However, many writers have pointed out (see Martin and Deutscher, Munsat, and Zemach) that this is at once too restrictive and too generous, ruling out obvious cases of memory and letting in cases that are equally obviously not cases of memory. On the one hand, Malcolm's account applies only where we know something from memory alone, and excludes those cases in which present experience confirms what we already know from memory; I certainly remember that there is a blackboard on the wall of my study, but I would know this fact even if I had not known it before, inasmuch as I now see the blackboard in front of me. On the other hand, I might see a partridge in a pear tree, tell a friend, and then forget all about it. He now tells me that last year I saw a partridge in a pear tree, so that it is true that I knew it before, that I know it now, and that if I had not known it before I would not know it now, since he can tell me about it only because I once told him. But this is still not remembering; rather, it is a case of learning it again.

More generally, it seems a mistake to suggest that knowledge in memory depends on past knowledge. My present knowledge that Brutus stabbed Caesar does not depend on previous knowledge that Brutus stabbed Caesar; it is precisely the same knowledge, which I still possess. Malcolm himself admits, ". . . it may be misleading to speak of *two* elements of knowledge in memory, previous and present knowledge. There are not two pieces but one piece. Memory is the *retention* of knowledge" (p. 229). But once we say that memory is the retention of knowledge, then, as Roger Squires argues ("Memory Unchained"), we do not need to think of the present knowledge as depending on the past knowledge. Retention, says Squires, is simply continuous possession. To say that the curtains have retained their color is not to say that their present color is dependent causally or, I would add, in any other way, on their past color; the curtains are not indigo now *because* they were indigo last year. It is simply to say that they still possess the color they once possessed. Similarly, to say that memory is retained

knowledge is only to say that it is knowledge possessed continuously from past acquisition up to
the time of remembering.

What Malcolm should have said is not that our
knowledge in memory is dependent on previous
knowledge, but that it is dependent, at least in
part, on previous acquisition. What makes my
knowledge that Brutus stabbed Caesar memory-
knowledge, is that it is knowledge acquired in the
past; and more importantly, to rule out cases in
which knowledge is acquired, forgotten, and then
acquired again, it is knowledge that I possess
now *because of* that past acquisition. This is
brought out most clearly by the special case of
being reminded of something that has been forgotten. When my friend tells me that I once saw
a partridge in a pear tree, I may be unable to remember it, and have to take his word for it—I
learn it again. But on the other hand I might
also remember it again, though I had forgotten
about it. How are we to distinguish the case in
which I now remember that I saw the partridge,
because I have been reminded of it, from the
case in which I cannot remember it at all, and
know that I saw it only because my friend as-
sures me I once told him about it? It seems that
the difference must lie in the fact that in one case
my present knowledge depends wholly on what
is now said, and so does not qualify as memory,
whereas in the other it also depends in part on the
earlier experience. This has the correct conse-

quence that insofar as you are unsure or cannot tell whether my present knowledge does depend on that earlier experience, you will also be unsure or unable to tell whether I really do remember it, as I claim to.

This point is made by Martin and Deutscher ("Remembering"), who argue also that the dependence must be a causal dependence, involving what can be called a "memory-trace," an internal state that provides a "structural analogue" for what is remembered, in the way that there is a structural analogy between musical sounds and the grooves in a phonograph record, for example. They are talking primarily about a form of personal memory, but I think they would argue generally that when a person remembers some fact, his original acquisition of the information will have produced in him a memory-trace that now produces his remembering, and it is in this way that the present remembering depends, causally, on the original acquisition. Many philosophers (e.g., Benjamin, Malcolm, Squires) argue against this that memory is not to be defined in terms of causal processes or mechanisms that somehow link past learning with present knowing. Perhaps memory may involve or be explained by some such physiological or neurological process, but, they insist, this is no part of what we mean by memory, of what we are talking about when we talk about remembering, any more than the secretion of digestive juices is part of what we mean by eating, even though this may be something that takes place when we eat. How could such things be part of what we mean, when as children we learn what memory and eating are long before we learn anything about neurological processes or digestive juices? Thus Malcolm says, "Whether or not it makes sense to postulate a specific brain-state or neural process persisting between the previous and present knowledge that p"—and Malcolm suggests it does not—"such a postulation is obviously not required by an analysis of the *concept* of remembering. Our everyday verifications of whether some person does or does not remember that p are not bound up with any questions about what is and has been going on in his brain. Our use of the language of memory carries no implications about inner physiology" ("Three Lectures on Memory," p. 237).

Now, Martin and Deutscher certainly agree that "the language of memory carries no implications about inner physiology." What is implicit in the language of memory, they say, is only that there be some form of causal link between past acquisition and present knowledge. Just what sort of link it is, whether it be an activity of the soul or a mechanism in the brain or an impression in the heart or a trace in the liver, is something that has to be established by scientific investigation. The way we talk about memory presupposes only that there be some such connection or another. There is not space here to go into the ingenious examples Martin and Deutscher produce, but personally I am not entirely convinced. For a start, although I would agree that in memory the present knowledge is, at least in part, dependent on previous acquisition, it does not follow that the dependence must be causal. Presumably, the dependence will be of the sort, whatever it may be, that usually holds between knowledge and the way it is acquired, and this does not seem to be a causal dependence. I know there is a book on my desk, because I see it there; the knowledge is thus dependent on the seeing; but it does not seem quite right to say that my seeing the book causes my knowledge that it is there.

Again, it is not clear whether memory necessarily involves memory-traces. Squires argues against this, saying that all that is necessary for factual memory is that factual knowledge be retained, i.e., possessed continuously, and for this we do not have to postulate persisting memory-traces. But there is one case discussed by Martin and Deutscher that raises a difficulty for Squires' account, and, more generally, for our definition of factual memory as retained factual knowledge. This, once again, is the case of being reminded. When I cannot remember someone's name for a long time, and then it comes back to me, it might be said that the knowledge was nevertheless continuously possessed, that I knew it all along even though I could not think of it. But if someone

reminds me of some fact I had completely forgotten, and would not have remembered if he
had not reminded me, it does not seem correct to
say that I possessed that knowledge continuously.
Something has been retained, something that enables me to say when reminded, "Ah yes, I remember it now." But that something does not
seem to be a piece of knowledge, because, before
I was reminded, I no longer knew the fact in
question.

Perhaps, then, factual memory is to be defined
not as retained factual knowledge, but, following
Martin and Deutscher, as knowledge that depends, at least in part, on something that might
be called a "memory-trace." There is a lot more to
be said about this question.

6

Practical Memory

Just as factual memory might be defined in terms of factual knowledge, so it seems that practical memory, remembering how to do something, can be defined in terms of practical knowledge, knowing how to do it. To remember how to drive a car is to know how to drive one, where this is not knowledge I have just acquired, but something I knew before; just as factual memory is retained factual knowledge, so, in the same way, practical memory is retained practical knowledge. And just as practical knowledge seems to consist in possessing certain acquired abilities and skills, so too does practical memory; to remember or know how to drive a car is simply to be able to do so. There do not seem to be any special problems here.

However Brian Smith has argued with some conviction (*Memory*, chap. V) that remembering how to do something is not simply a matter of being able to do it, but is more a matter of knowing what to do, of knowing that certain things have to be done—as knowing how to drive this particular car involves knowing that the starter button is on the floor, not on the dashboard. This may not affect the definition of practical memory in terms of practical knowledge, since I suspect that Smith would say the same things about knowing how to do something that he says about remembering how to do it, but if Smith is correct remembering how would seem to reduce to a form of remembering that, which would mean that practical memory is not a separate form of memory distinct from factual memory.

Smith argues that we can speak of someone remembering how to do something even when he is not doing it and is perhaps unable to do it; and conversely, someone may be able to do or even actually do something without our wanting to say that he is remembering how to do it. On the one hand, the mere fact that the lizard can catch flies does not mean that it remembers how to do so. Smith suggests that this shows that a purely automatic response cannot count as remembering how, but the explanation might rather be that we speak of remembering how only where we are referring to skills that have had to be acquired, more particularly skills that have to be acquired outside the normal process of development—we do not speak of remembering how to breathe, or even how to walk, as we do speak of remembering how to ride a bicycle. Nevertheless, Smith insists that someone who is doing, in a completely automatic manner, something he has learned to do, is not remembering how to do it. Certainly I am not, at this particular moment, remembering how to type, even though I am typing. On the other hand, an arthritic diver may remember how to execute some particularly complicated dive, and may pass the information on to a young champion, even though he is no longer capable of doing it himself. Again, as Smith points out, there are occasions on which we have to remember how to do something *before* we can do it, which surely suggests that the two are different—I may, for example, have to stop and think how to tie a running bowline in order to be able to tie one.

So, Smith insists, remembering how to do something and being able to do it, or even actually doing it, are different, though the two may come together: "While I am sitting at my desk I may run through in my mind all those rules, maxims and propositions (which may be classified as 'how to drive a car'). To do this would be to actualize my disposition *to remember how* to drive a car. On the other hand I may, on a long, straight, lonely road, sit back at the wheel of a car allowing my mind to wander while my hands and feet respond automatically to the feel of the car beneath me and the sight of the road ahead, and then I would be actualising my dispositional ability *to make the efficient physical manoeuvres* which constitute the overt performance. But, when I am driving through the town, easing the clutch, touching the brake, marking to whom I must give way and who must give way to me . . . , etc., . . . then, unless I am an extremely practised driver, I am actualising both dispositions together" (*Memory*, p. 128).

I think there are two important distinctions that Smith fails to make in this argument. The first is that between occurrent and non-occurrent uses of the word "remember." It is clear that Smith is concentrating on the occurrent use; he is considering what is involved in actively remembering, at some particular point in time, how to do something. Now it is not at all clear to me that there are acts or occurrences of remembering how, in the way that there are acts or occurrences of remembering that, e.g., I have left the gas on. Personally I am not much tempted to say, when I am driving carefully and deliberately, that I am there and then remembering how to drive the car. Nevertheless, if anything does count as actively remembering, at a point in time, how to do something, then it will, as Smith argues, consist in going over in one's mind the various performances involved and the rules and maxims that govern them—and it is in this sense that someone who cannot himself do something might nevertheless be said to remember how to do it. But although occurrences of remembering how, if there are such occurrences, may reduce in this way to occurrences of remembering various facts about what to do and how to do it, the same is not true of non-occurrent remembering how. I remember how to ride a bicycle, as is demonstrated by the fact that, when put on one, I ride away without falling off, even though I do not, and cannot, formulate, in speech or thought, precisely what I do in order to remain on top of the bike. This shows not that I do not remember how to ride a bicycle, but that I am unable to remember how in any occurrent sense of "remember how." Riding a bicycle is not an occurrence or act of remembering how to do it, any more than walking straight to my parked car is an act or occurrence of remembering that this is where I parked it. But both count as remembering in the non-occurrent sense of the word.

The second distinction is between remembering how to do something and remembering how it is done, both of which might be called "remembering how." There is a sense in which, for example, I remember how to play a trumpet—you blow down the thin end and twiddle the knobs—but I certainly do not remember or know how to play one in the sense of being able to do so. Now it is in this sense, of knowing how it is done, that the arthritic diver remembers how to perform the complicated dive even though he can no longer perform it himself; and it is in this sense that I have to remember how to tie a running bowline before I can manage to tie one. So it seems that when Smith talks about occurrences of remembering how, he is thinking specifically of remembering how something is done—and this, I would agree, is a form of factual memory. But if we distinguish remembering how to do something from remembering how it is done, and if we restrict the label "practical memory" to the former, which consists in the possession of some previously acquired skill or ability, then practical memory is not reducible to a form of factual memory.

Smith's argument shows that "remembering how" can cover remembering how something is done, which is a form of factual memory, as well as practical memory proper; and that occurrences of remembering how something is done—i.e., specific acts of bringing to mind the fact that you do x by doing a, b, c, etc.—consist in occurrences of factual memory. But this does not show that occurrences of practical memory proper consist in occurrences of factual memory, if indeed there are such things as specific occurrences of practical memory, particular acts of remembering how to do something, in the first place.

7

Personal Memory

Personal memory is the memory we have of particular items—people, places, things, events, situations—that we have personally experienced. It is in this way that I remember Vienna, because I have been there, but not Hong Kong; that I remember yesterday's meeting, but not the Napoleonic Wars, because they were before my time. The distinctive feature of this form of memory is not that it is memory of specific items as opposed to memory of facts and skills; we sometimes speak of remembering specific items without it being personal memory that is involved. In reciting a list of African capitals, I may remember Accra and forget Cairo, but remembering Accra is not personal memory, because I have never been there. The distinctive feature of personal memory is that it is memory of items that you have experienced for yourself, in the loose and broad sense of "experience" in which I experienced the Second World War because I lived through it, even though I did not see any battles, hear any guns, or feel any explosions.

However, Ayer has argued that it is only a contingent fact that what I am calling personal memory is restricted to what we have personally experienced, since it is at least logically possible that we might remember the experiences of others (see *Problem of Knowledge,* pp. 144–45). If Ayer is right, then perhaps we should modify our account to say that personal memory is memory of things *as if* you have experienced them for yourself, but I am not sure that he is right. Certainly, a person could have knowledge and imagery of something he had not experienced, just as if he had experienced it, and it might turn out to be just the knowledge and imagery as was once possessed by someone else who did experience it. But the question is whether we would describe this as *remembering.* I think we would prefer to speak of clairvoyance or telepathy, or of his seeming to remember, rather than of his actually remembering it. A person can seem to remember something he did not experience, just as he can seem to remember something that did not happen, but seeming to remember is not itself remembering, and I do not think we would call it remembering proper unless the man had experienced it for himself. Of course, this may be only a verbal point, a point about the restrictions we place on the legitimate use of the verb "remember," but nevertheless it seems to me correct; personal memory is restricted to those cases in which the claim to remember something incorporates a claim to have experienced it.

Personal memory is, once again, parallel to a form of knowledge; just as we speak of remembering a person or place we have had personal experience of, so we speak of knowing a person or place we have had personal experience of. So it might seem that, just as factual and practical memory can be defined in terms of factual and practical knowledge, so too personal memory can be defined in terms of personal knowledge; just as factual memory is factual knowledge that has been acquired in the past, so personal memory is personal knowledge in which the personal experience lies in the past. But this is not so. For a start, we do not speak of knowing an incident, scene, or situation in the way that we speak of remembering an incident, scene, or situation; and it could be argued that we remember people or places only insofar as we remember incidents, scenes, or situations involving those people or places. And second, remembering a person or place does not always amount to knowing that person or place. There is a certain minimum acquaintance necessary before we can claim to know someone, but the same minimum does not apply to remembering him. Merely shaking hands with Lord Bloggs at a civic function is not sufficient for the claim to know him, but it is sufficient for me to remember him. Similarly, I once spent two days in New York and I remember it well, but I would hardly claim to know New York, let alone to know it well.

Perhaps, then, personal memory is to be defined in terms of factual memory, and so in terms of factual knowledge; to remember some item x is to remember, and so to know, facts about x, which you have experienced for yourself. But this will not do as it stands, since I might remember many facts about things I experienced as a child, because my parents have told me about them, and yet not be able to remember those things themselves. So we might say instead, to remember some item x is to remember, and so to know, facts about x, because you have experienced it for yourself. But even this will not do. I have always remembered that as a child I traveled in an airplane, and I have remembered this fact ever since it happened—I even reminded my parents of it when they had forgotten. So I remember, and know, that as a child I traveled in an airplane, and I know this fact because I experienced that flight. But I cannot remember the flight; I can remember that it happened, but I cannot remember it. It seems, then, that if I am to remember some item, I must not only remember *that* it happened or existed or that I experienced it, etc., but also remember *what* it was like, i.e., I must remember something about it. If I could remember that I sat next to an old lady in a blue dress and that I was very sick and scared, for example, then I could be said to remember the flight, and the more I remember about it, the better I remember it. So, it seems, personal memory is to be explained in terms of factual knowledge of what that which I experienced was like, where I know this because I experienced it.

But now there is the difficulty that we often remember things incorrectly, and if this is so, how can personal memory be defined in terms of knowledge? It is usually said to this that the word "remember," like the word "know," is truth-entailing, i.e., that "I remember p," like "I know p," but unlike "I think p" or "I believe p," entails the truth of p. If p is false, then we should say not "I remember p," but "As I remember it, p" or "p is how I remember it," for these latter expressions do not entail the correctness of p. But it seems to me that "remember" is normally truth-entailing only when we are speaking of factual memory. I cannot remember that the Battle of Hastings was fought in 1173 any more than I can know it; I might think or believe it, but I cannot be said to remember or know it unless it is a fact. But there is not the same restriction on "remember" when we are speaking of personal memory; I can say, for example, "I remember John breaking the window, but I now learn to my surprise that it was Tom who did it." On the other hand, I would agree with Malcolm that we cannot speak of remembering if the memory is *totally* incorrect. I might be said to remember John breaking the window when in fact it was Tom, but I cannot be said to remember a visit to Hong Kong if I have never been near the place. I might think or claim that I remember it, but I would be mistaken; if my memory is wrong not just in details, but about the very occurrence of such a thing, then we would say that my memory is delusive and I do not remember it at all. As Malcolm says, "A totally delusive memory is no more a memory than a fictitious occurrence is something that happened, or no more than a painted fire is a fire. This is not mere quibbling. A painted fire does not have the important properties of fire and a totally delusive memory does not have the important properties of memory" ("Three Lectures on Memory," p. 191). So although personal memory can be incorrect in some respects, it must also be correct in others if it is to count as memory rather than imagination in the first place. Personal memory must involve some factual knowledge of what is remembered, even if some of the things we think we remember did not happen, at least not as we remember them.

There is a further, and I think conclusive, objection to any attempt to define personal memory in terms of factual knowledge: personal memory does not necessarily involve knowing that it did happen or that it was experienced. As in our earlier example, a man may have what he takes to be a recurring fantasy of having been kidnaped, when in fact this actually happened to him and he is, without knowing it, remembering it. Here he remembers being kidnaped and yet knows nothing about that kidnaping because he thinks that no such thing ever happened. We can avoid this difficulty if we say, as Malcolm does, that he remembers the kidnaping only to the extent that he can also be said to remember that he was seized by three masked men, put in a green car, and so on. But then, as we saw, this itself constitutes an objection to the definition, which Malcolm himself adopts, of factual memory in terms of factual knowledge: if he remembers that he was seized, etc., nevertheless he does not know, or even believe, that he was. So either way, whether we say that he remembers *that* he was seized, etc., or not, the fact remains that he remembers being kidnaped without knowing that he was kidnaped. In this case, personal memory does not involve factual knowledge of something we have experienced for ourselves.

Rather, it seems that personal memory consists in bringing some previously experienced thing to mind, thinking about it again, and going over what it was like, whether we realize that we have actually experienced it or not, where the ability to do this depends on our having experienced it. No doubt the dependence will be of the same sort, whatever that may be, that we discussed in connection with factual memory. And this, as we have seen, is how the traditional theories describe memory, as bringing some previously experienced thing back to mind, or perhaps as experiencing it again. It is, as I suggested at the end of chapter 4, personal memory that the traditional theories of memory were intended to explain. As Broad says, this "is the one and only kind of memory which can plausibly be regarded as closely analogous to perception" (*Mind and Its Place in Nature*, p. 222), and for this reason he calls it not "personal," but "perceptual" memory. So our next task is to consider how far those traditional theories are accurate, if not as theories of remembering in general, at least as theories of personal memory in particular.

8

The Traditional Theories Reconsidered

In chapter 4 we saw that both the Representative and the Realist theories of memory are based on three central claims about remembering: that it is or involves an act or occurrence; that this occurrence is a mental experience, involving mental imagery; and that this occurrence provides a source of knowledge. We saw that these claims are all false of memory in general, but the question now is whether and how far they are true of personal memory in particular.

Certainly "remember" has both an occurrent and a non-occurrent use when used of personal memory, just as it has in other cases. I can be said to remember my twenty-first birthday even when I am fast asleep or absorbed in a book. But in this case, unlike factual or practical memory, it seems that the general ability to remember is an ability to perform particular acts of remembering, of bringing back to mind various scenes and incidents that have been experienced in the past. So it might be said that personal memory does essentially involve specific acts or occurrences of remembering, in a way that factual and practical memory do not.

But are these occurrences special mental occurrences that involve mental imagery? Certainly we often have imagery when we remember things we have experienced, but is this necessarily so? Can we remember something in this way, without forming an image of it? It seems we can. If, for example, someone can describe the shops in the main street of his home town, but insists that he cannot form images of how they looked, we will still say that he remembers those shops. If Evans can remember that Jones the Draper's was a musty old Victorian shop, between Thomas the Butcher and Morgan the Baker, remarkable mainly for Jones's beautiful daughter, and so on, then we will say that he remembers Jones the Draper's well, irrespective of whether he has images when he remembers these things. (For further examples, see Malcolm, "Three Lectures on Memory," p. 206; Martin and Deutscher, "Remembering," p. 165.) This shows that a detailed account of something we have experienced can count as personal memory of that thing, and that going over what we thus remember, either overtly or "in our minds," can qualify as an occurrence of personal remembering. Having an image of something is one way of remembering it, but it is not the only way. Another way is to describe it, or perhaps draw it, informing others or reminding ourselves of what it was like. As Ryle says, "Reminiscence in imagery does not differ in principle [from such overt performances as describing or physically depicting the remembered thing] though it tends to be superior in speed, if otherwise greatly inferior in efficiency" (*Concept of Mind*, p. 275).

However this is not the end of the matter. When we talk about remembering some specific item in this way we can distinguish between recalling the item itself and recalling various facts about that item, both of which can qualify as personal memory. That is, there is a difference between remembering what something was like in the sense of remembering that it was such-and-such, and remembering what it was like in the sense of remembering the such-and-suchness of it; and I do not think a person can be said to recall an item, as opposed to recalling facts about it, unless he remembers what it was like in this latter sense. Someone who remembers that a certain shop was dark, dirty, and musty may be said to remember the shop, even to remember it well, but I do not think he can be said to recall it unless he remembers not just that it was dark, dirty, and musty, but remembers the dark, the dirt, the musty smell. Now this, it seems to me, is precisely what it is to have a memory-image of something; when I remember the dark, the dirt, the musty smell of that shop, as opposed merely to remembering that it was dark, dirty, and musty, then I am having memory-images of it. And if this is so— if recalling a thing as opposed to recalling facts about it is tantamount to having memory-images of it—then the recollection of particular items essentially involves mental imagery. In other words, although personal memory, in the sense of remembering particular things we have experienced, may be possible without mental imagery, the recollection of such things is not. So the traditional theories may be correct, after all, as accounts of that particular, and I think most characteristic, form of personal memory which involves recalling the remembered thing.

Moreover, I think there is now a fairly straightforward explanation of how traditional theorists came to concentrate on this particular type of remembering, to the exclusion not only of quite different forms of memory such as factual and practical memory, but also of other forms of personal memory. Our recollections of particular items are sometimes described as *memories:* a memory is some previously experienced item as we recall it; to be left with our memories is to be left with our recollections of things from our past; and to recount those memories is to describe those things as we remember them. So the basic error of the traditional theories may well be the failure to distinguish between memory in this sense, in which we talk of "a memory" and "memories," and memory in the sense of our general ability to remember. Certainly, most discussions of memory, traditional and contemporary, do not notice the distinction, and it seems obvious that the traditional theories are best interpreted not as theories of memory in general, of our ability to remember, but as theories of memories, of what it is to recall some particular thing that we have experienced.

The final question is whether personal memory, or more particularly our memories, can be said to provide a source of knowledge. Once again, it seems not. I remember Vienna, and in remembering Vienna I know various facts about Vienna, but my remembering Vienna is hardly what provides me with this information. I acquired my knowledge of Vienna not by remembering Vienna, but by walking its streets and visiting its monuments; the source of my knowledge, the way I come to know the various facts, is not my present remembering, but my previous visit. (The point is well made by Ryle in *Concept of Mind,* p. 274.)

Nevertheless, there are some rather special circumstances in which personal memory, in particular the recollection of specific items, might be said to be the source of knowledge, to be what provides us with information. Suppose, for example, I am asked whether Smith is bald, and I am not sure. I then recall how he looks, and decide that, yes, he is bald. Here is a case in which I come to know some fact by recalling a particular item, and insofar as recalling that item involves having a memory-image of it, it is also a case in which a memory-image provides me with knowledge. Some philosophers (e.g., R. F. Holland, "The Empiricist Theory of Memory," p. 485) have argued against this possibility on the grounds that we cannot remember how things were, not even in the form of having a memory-image, unless we already know how they were and so know how to form the appropriate image, but I think this exaggerates the extent to which imagery has to be voluntary and deliberate. Often our images occur whether we want them or not; there are those terrible scenes we just cannot get out of our minds. And just as imagery is not always voluntary and deliberate, so we do not always actively construct our memory images in order to illustrate what we already know to be the case.

It might be said, however, that the source of knowledge in our example is nevertheless not the present memory but the previous experience; I know that Smith is bald, only because I once met him. Now, certainly I remember him as bald only because I have seen his bald head, but it does not follow that my seeing his bald head is the source of my present knowledge, for it may be that I have forgotten the fact in the meantime. To take a clearer example, someone may ask me whether I have seen Smith recently, and I say I have not. An hour later, with a shock, I remember talking to him only yesterday. How do I now know that I saw him yesterday, when an hour ago I did not know it? Because I now recall talking to him. Surely here it is the present remembering that provides me with the knowledge, knowledge I did not have an hour back. Indeed, to take an even more extreme example, it seems that personal memory can provide us with knowledge that has not merely been forgotten, but was not previously possessed at all. To go back to an earlier example (p. 54 above), I may be asked whether a certain student was present at my lecture, and come to know that he was present, though I did not realize it at the time, because now—and only now, when I think back over the lecture—I can recall him sitting in the back row. My imagery here does not depend on previous knowledge, because I did not know he was there until I had the imagery. Rather, my knowledge depends on memory, in that it is only because I now recall him sitting there that I know that he was present. Once again memory, personal memory, is a source of knowledge.

But these obviously are rather special cases. It would be most implausible to generalize from them and claim that personal memory is the source of all memory-knowledge. However, we can interpret the claim that personal memory provides us with knowledge in a weaker and more favorable way. So far I have taken the claim to be that memory is a "source" of knowledge, something that provides us with information we would not otherwise have known. But we might take the claim to be that memory, in particular personal memory, provides us with the "evidence" or justification that can turn true belief into knowledge. One of the things that most concerns us in the theory of knowledge is the question of grounds or evidence. When we assert that someone knows something, we are, among other things, asserting that something is true, is the case; and when the assertion of knowledge is challenged, one of the things we have to do is to produce evidence that what is said to be known is indeed the case. This, in philosophical discussion and in ordinary conversation, is often the point of the question "How do you know?," and we can define "evidence" in the sense in which I am using the term as anything that provides an answer to the question asked in this way, i.e., anything that shows or helps to show that what is said to be known is in fact true. Evidence in this sense also constitutes grounds, in that anything that indicates something is true is also at the same time a reason for believing that it is true. Now I am suggesting that the claim that personal memory provides us with knowledge might be taken to mean not that it is a source of knowledge, but that it provides or constitutes evidence that what we claim to know is indeed the case, and thus provides or constitutes at least part of the grounds for believing that it is the case.

After all, the most obvious reason for insisting that memory can and does provide us with knowledge is the fact that it is often an entirely sensible and adequate answer to the question of how I know something, to say that I remember it. How do I know that John broke his leg? Because I remember him breaking it. Now my remembering him break his leg is not the source of my knowledge that he did; it is not what provides me with the information that John broke his leg. I know that it happened because I was there at the time and saw it happen, and this is part of what I claim when I claim to remember him breaking his leg. But although my remembering it happen is not the source of my knowledge, it is certainly evidence that John did break his leg. It is, in fact, just the sort of evidence that law courts like to rely on. Notice, however, that although personal memory can provide evidence that what I claim to know is true, it need not be that my own belief is grounded on that evidence. I probably believe it already, without appealing to the evidence of my memories. Or, in other cases, I might be unsure about what happened, and in that case my memories could provide grounds for my own belief: it may be only because I dimly remember, through an alcoholic haze, throwing a bottle and the sound of tinkling glass, that I believe that I broke a window.

Notice, too, that the evidence in these cases is not that I remember *that* it happened, but that I remember it happening. It would be no explanation of how I know that Napoleon died on St. Helena to say that I remember that he did. This is merely to repeat that I know it, not to explain how I know it. Factual memory does not provide evidence or grounds for believing, because, as we have seen, factual memory is already a type of knowledge; in this case, to remember it *is* to know it. But it would be very different if I were to remember Napoleon dying on St. Helena; that would indeed be evidence that he did die there. Personal memory can provide evidence or grounds because, as we have also seen, personal memory is not itself knowledge. To remember something happening is not to know it any more than to see it happen is to know it, but both seeing and remembering can provide grounds for believing that it did happen, for accepting some fact as a fact, and so for accepting it as knowledge. Personal memory is not typically a source of knowledge, but it does, typically, provide us with evidence in support of our claims to know various things.

So, to sum up, although the traditional theories may be inadequate as theories of memory in general, they do seem fairly accurate as theories of personal memory specifically. For first, personal memory does seem to require occurrences of remembering, of bringing back to mind various items that we have experienced in the past. Second, although not all personal memory involves imagery, it can be argued that our memories, i.e., our recollections of particular items as opposed to recalling facts about those items, do essentially involve mental imagery. And finally, personal memory can provide us with knowledge, both in that it sometimes provides us with information we would not otherwise have known, and also and more characteristically in that it provides evidence in support of what we claim to know. Philosophers in the past have almost universally accepted these traditional theories, because they failed to distinguish personal from other forms of memory, more especially because they failed to distinguish memory in general from *a* memory.

Precisely the same mistake is made by those contemporary philosophers who insist that memory is but a form of knowledge, and so cannot be something that provides us with knowledge. (Many of the points above are discussed in more detail in my "Memory, Memories and Me.")

Now, with this partial rehabilitation of the traditional approach, our next question must be which of the two classic theories is in fact the correct one, construed as a theory of personal memory, or memories, in particular. I think that the Representative theory has been the most widely held because of the common view that, as Von Leyden puts it, "we remember, strictly speaking, no more than our past perceptions of things" (*Remembering*, p. 65). Some such view is certainly implicit in the storehouse analogies suggested by Locke and St. Augustine (see p. 4 above). The fundamental idea behind the Representative theory seems to be that when we remember some previously experienced thing, we reproduce, or perhaps produce again, in our minds not that thing itself but our original experience of it. E. J. Furlong goes even further and suggests, most implausibly, that what we recall is our total state of mind at the time when we originally experienced the remembered item (*A Study in Memory*, pp. 75–77). Yet the fact is that often, when we remember, our memory image is not the same as the original experience. I might, for example, remember falling down some stairs, but when I remember it I "see" it, in my image, as if I were a spectator watching myself fall. This could not possibly have been my experience at the time. Clearly, then, our images in remembering are not the original experiences produced again, nor even present reproductions or representations of those original experiences.

What is true is that we can remember only those things we have experienced for ourselves, and we can recall them only to the extent that we did experience them. I can remember the coronation of Elizabeth II, although I was not present at the ceremony, inasmuch as I remember the flags in the streets and the patriotic speeches; and when I remember the coronation, it is those particular things I did witness that I recall. But this does not mean that I recall those things as I originally perceived them, much less that I recall the original perceptions themselves. There is no special support here for the Representative theory. Nor is it correct to say, as Brian Smith does (*Memory*, p. 89), that remembering an event amounts to remembering perceiving that event. The two are different: I might remember something I have seen without remembering where or when I saw it. Conversely, I might remember seeing someone killed in a traffic accident, without, because of the shock perhaps, being able to remember what I saw—just as I can remember meeting someone without remembering what he was like.

It seems to me that the choice between the

Representative and the Realist theories of memory will have to turn on our interpretation of the mental imagery involved in recalling specific items. For this, at bottom, is the point at issue between the two: the Representative theorist thinks of the memory-image as a present representation of the past item; the Realist thinks of the memory-image as that past item itself, as it appears to us in our remembering. So, for the Representative theorist, memory-images will be mental entities, such as, for example, a mental picture we are aware of in some way that is at least analogous to the ways in which we perceive physical objects. But for the Realist, images are not entities at all, but rather "a certain mode of awareness, the way an object appears when it enters into a memory situation" (Woozley, as quoted on p. 24 above).

Now, if we once think of images as entities we perceive, we are immediately faced with a host of insoluble problems. Where are they? What are they made of? How do we perceive them? We certainly do not perceive images in anything like the way we perceive objects in the world around us, nor are images at all like pictures or any other sort of perceptual object. We cannot go into the difficult and fascinating topic of imagery here, but it is significant that many philosophers want to replace the "entity" conception of images, which gives rise to all these problems, by what we might call a "process" conception (for references, see the bibliography). That is, rather than talk of mental images as mysterious entities that we are in some equally mysterious way aware of, we might talk about a process or activity of visualizing (for visual imagery) or more generally of "imaging." Perhaps the exact nature of this process remains mysterious, but at least we then have but one mystery, where before we had two. This approach seems to me to have much to commend it, and if we adopt it, as many contemporary philosophers seem prepared to, then we are committed to a Realist theory. For on this view of imagery, to talk about memory-images will be to talk not about present representations of past events, but to talk about a special sort of imagination-awareness of past events themselves. If images are not entities, they are not representations; if talk about imagery is talk about a certain sort of awareness, then talk about memory-images will be talk about a certain sort of awareness of the past. "Once we reject the 'entity' view of imagery we simply cannot maintain that *an image* is a symbol or a sign either of a past event or of a kind or class of entities. What we contemplate when we image is the appearance presented by the past event itself" (Brian Smith, *Memory*, p. 168). So, insofar as I personally am drawn toward this account of mental imagery, I personally prefer the Realist theory as a theory of memories—of what it is to recall some specific item that one has previously experienced.

9
Memory-Knowledge

We saw that one of the standard difficulties for
the traditional theories of memory is that they
seem to provide no way of telling when we are
remembering and when we are not—when we are
merely and mistakenly *thinking* we remember. In
that case, memory could never provide us with
knowledge, and there could be no such thing as
memory-knowledge. This question, of whether
memory can ever enable us to know anything,
is one of the major topics in the philosophy of
memory, and to it we now turn. But it will help
if, at the outset, we notice that the label "memory-
knowledge" covers more than one thing. Once
we have distinguished between personal memory
and factual memory, we can also distinguish between our knowledge of the things we remember
and our memory of facts we already know, i.e.,
between memory-knowledge in the sense of
knowledge of things experienced in the past, and
memory-knowledge in the sense of knowledge
acquired in the past and since retained. If we fail
to distinguish the two forms of memory there
will be a constant temptation to assimilate one

form of memory-knowledge to the other, to think either that all memory-knowledge will be knowledge based on what we personally remember, or that memory-knowledge is merely retained knowledge and as such not dependent on personal memory at all (as instances of the two extremes, see Von Leyden, *Remembering*, p. 65, and Ryle, *Concept of Mind*, p. 274). But neither of these views is entirely right.

Thus, we saw in the last chapter that personal memory can provide us with knowledge, most characteristically in that it provides evidence that various things have happened or did exist, but also occasionally in the stronger sense that it provides the rememberer with information he would not otherwise have known. But not all memory-knowledge depends on memory in these ways. I remember that Harold was killed at Hastings, but I have no memories that inform me of this fact, nor can I recall anything that might serve as evidence for it. No doubt I read or was told of it somewhere, and I might have one or two books that, I am sure, would prove the point if someone disputed it. But at the moment I cannot recall anything that shows that Harold was killed at Hastings, as I remember he was. Whatever this memory-knowledge depends on, it certainly does not depend on any element of personal memory. Indeed, usually when we speak of knowing some fact "from memory," this means not that our memory tells us something we did not know, but precisely that we knew it already. When I say I know it "from memory," I explain not *how* I know it, but *what sort of* knowledge it is; I explain that it is knowledge I acquired in the past and have so far managed to retain. Similarly when it is said that most human knowledge depends on memory, what is meant is not that memory provides us with most of the information we know, but that most of our knowledge depends on our ability to retain information that we have acquired. Memory, here, is not the *acquisition* of knowledge, but the *retention* of knowledge; and, as Sydney Shoemaker says, "If it can be denied that knowledge and belief can be simply retained, and that a belief can be well grounded simply in virtue of having been acquired on the basis of good evidence or from a reliable source, the only alternative seems to be that we must be constantly *re*acquiring, on the basis of a continuous supply of fresh evidence, every item of knowledge we possess and are said to remember. The latter seems a fantastic view, yet it appears to be implicit in the representative theory and other classical theories of memory" ("Memory," pp. 271–72).

How, then, did philosophers come to adopt this fantastic view that whenever we remember some fact, there must be some present memory-experience that informs us of it? I think there are two factors at work here. First of all, it is said that I know some fact because I learned it in the past; I know that it rained yesterday, because I was outside at the time and got wet. But, it might be argued, although this explains how I originally came to know it, it does not explain how I know it *now*, for I often forget things I have learned. I have no idea whether or not it rained a year ago, so what explains how I know now that it rained yesterday, when in a year's time I probably will not know it? I know that it rained yesterday because I remember it raining, so although my getting wet explained my knowledge at the time, it is my present remembering that accounts for my present knowledge.

In this way, we get two questions, the question of how someone knows a certain fact in the first place, and the question of how he knows it at some later point in time. And once we distinguish the two questions, we can see how it might be thought that all memory-knowledge rests on memory-experiences, particularly if we adopt the empiricist view that all knowledge comes from experience. For if all knowledge comes from experience, then if I know some fact it must be because I have experienced something that informs me of that fact; and similarly, if I know some fact now, as opposed to knowing it a year ago, there must be some present experience that informs me of it, and presumably this will be the memory-experience. But, fairly clearly, one of our two questions is bogus, or at best not a philosophical one. To explain how someone knows a certain fact in the first place is also to explain how he knows it at a later point in time. I know now that Harold was killed at Hastings because I have retained my previous knowledge of that fact. I do not know how I originally learned it, and to say I remember it is not to explain how I know it now, but simply to say that I have retained the information. Of course, there is the question of how we manage to retain information, and equally the question of how we come to forget things we have learned, but the answers to these questions lie in psychology or neurology, not in the philosophy of mind or the theory of knowledge. Thus, the theory that memory is the source of all memory-knowledge arises, in part, as an answer to a non-existent problem, the problem of what informs me of some fact at the time when I remember that fact. The truth is that where a fact is remembered, i.e., retained, there is nothing, and no need of anything, that now informs me of that fact.

A second factor that may lead to the suggestion that memory-knowledge is knowledge for which memory provides evidence, is this. It is usually said that if a person is to know some fact, his knowledge must be based on grounds or evidence that what he claims to know is in fact true; knowledge is *justified* true belief. So if memory-knowledge is knowledge acquired in the past, then, it seems, its grounds will be remembered grounds, as my ground for insisting that John broke his leg is that I remember him breaking it. All knowledge requires evidence or grounds; memory-knowledge is knowledge that has been acquired in the past; therefore, the grounds or evidence for memory-knowledge must be remembered grounds or evidence. Thus, all memory-knowledge will be knowledge for which memory provides evidence. But this too is a mistake, and one that has interesting consequences for the general theory of knowledge. I remember that Harold was killed at Hastings, yet I can remember nothing that serves as evidence for this fact. What this shows is that a man can remember, and so know, some fact without having, at that particular time, any evidence that it is a fact. Insofar as memory-knowledge is knowledge acquired in the past, it is knowledge for which the evidence or grounds lies in the past, and may have been forgotten. When we speak "strictly from memory," what we mean is precisely that we remember, or think we remember, some fact without remembering anything that shows it to be true. So the claim that in order to know a fact a man must have evidence that it is a fact, has to be modified. The most that can be claimed is that he must *have had* evidence for it, for a man may very well know something without knowing how he knows it, as is the case with my knowledge that Harold was killed at Hastings.

It is, then, an error to think that memory-knowledge must be knowledge that depends on memory, either in the sense in which memory is its source or in the sense in which memory provides evidence for the truth of what is known. There are many facts we remember without being able to appeal to personal memory for their support. But, equally, it is an error to think that memory-knowledge can only be knowledge that is retained from past acquisition, without depending in any way on present remembering. There are some facts we know that are supported by what we personally remember, and even, occasionally, facts we know only because of what we personally remember. To avoid confusion here, we have to distinguish between two kinds of memory-knowledge, between factual memory-knowledge (knowledge we retain or remember) and personal memory-knowledge (knowledge based, at least in part, on what we personally remember). The two overlap, of course—my knowledge that it rained yesterday is both remembered knowledge and knowledge based on personal memory—but it is a mistake to concentrate on one to the exclusion of the other.

Thus, for example, Shoemaker maintains, "Scepticism about memory, if it is distinct from scepticism about knowledge in general, is scepticism about the retention of knowledge," and argues that since there could not be knowledge or belief at all unless knowledge and belief were retained, there are in fact no skeptical problems about memory in particular, apart from the general problem of whether we know what we think we know ("Memory," pp. 273–74). But this, of course, is to ignore skepticism about personal memory—the question whether we can legitimately claim to know that the things we remember happening did happen. Holland takes an opposite tack and seems to ignore factual memory-knowledge in favor of personal memory-knowledge, when he suggests that it is misleading or even incorrect to say that such things as chains of inference, scientific conclusions, or color judgments "rest on memory": "When asked which of two fabrics is Pea Green and which is Apple Green, I may succeed in remembering. . . . That both are *green* I can neither remember nor forget. The supposition that all scientific conclusions and all judgements about colour rest on memory, if it is not to be simply false, involves the use of the word 'memory' in an esoteric and dubious sense" ("The Empiricist Theory of Memory," p. 477). Certainly, such knowledge does not depend on personal memory; I may have to recall an apple in order to decide whether the fabric is pea green or apple green, but I do not have to recall anything in order to tell that this color is green. But this does not show that my knowing what green is is not memory-knowledge, in the sense of remembered knowledge. That this color is green, that the premises of the argument were such and such, that this conclusion was drawn from the data, these are all pieces of information that I retain from past acquisition, even though I know them without having to recall that past acquiring.

Incidentally, with this distinction between two types of memory-knowledge we can now deal with a difficulty that remains from our discussion of factual memory. On p. 54 above, I suggested a case that did not fit our definition of factual memory as retained factual knowledge: on recalling the audience at my lecture, I now realize for the first time that a certain student was there, after all; I remember that he was there, but this is not a case of retained knowledge, because up till now, I did not know it at all. We can now see that this is an example of personal memory-knowledge that is not factual memory-knowledge; it is not factual memory at all, so we should not expect our definition of factual memory to cover it. What we have here is not a remembered fact, but a fact about a remembered thing (I think we could deal with Malcolm's cases of "impure" factual memory, p. 54 above, in the same way).

This example shows that the "remember that" construction need not always indicate a case of factual memory—as we have said before, grammar provides but a rough guide to the type of memory in question. There are in fact two different, though normally overlapping, ways in which we use this expression; we can use it to report remembered facts, as in "I remember that Harold was killed at Hastings," or we can use it to describe items or incidents that we remember, as in "I remember that Uncle Tom got drunk and spilled beer all over Aunt Matilda." Indeed, of the two, I think the latter is the more common and more natural use of the expression. Most philosophical talk about memory is, of necessity, not particularly idiomatic, and we do not normally say things like "I remember that E = mc²" or "I remember that this color is green," though there is not the same oddity about "I remember what color green is." In reporting what we know or remember, we usually drop the words "I know" or "I remember," and simply report the facts. As Benjamin points out ("Remembering," pp. 327–31), "I remember" in such contexts, like "I know," serves to certify what is said to be remembered or known; roughly speaking, "I remember that p," like "I know that p," amounts to "p, and you have my word for it." But, typically, we do not bother to back up our assertions in this way.

So if we distinguish a fact-stating from a memory-describing use of "remember that," it seems to be the latter that is the more common, the more idiomatic. This is interesting, for it might be argued that the memory-describing use, unlike the fact-stating use, is not necessarily truth-entailing. We have seen that I cannot be said to remember some fact unless it is a fact, but we have also seen that personal memory is not always or necessarily correct in all its details, and that we can speak of remembering things, as opposed to facts, that did not happen. In such a case, we might well claim to remember that something happened when it did not; perhaps Uncle Tom never got drunk in his life, let alone spilled beer over Aunt Matilda. I agree that it is arguable whether one can legitimately use the "remember that" construction even in a case like this, but perhaps the fact that it is arguable explains why some philosophers have wanted to suggest that there is a non-truth-entailing use of "remember," even though it is clearly not legitimate to say that someone remembers that the Battle of Hastings was fought in 1173.

10

Is Memory Reliable?

If there is to be such a thing as memory-knowledge, we will need some way of telling whether the facts we remember are indeed facts —whether the things we remember happening did actually happen. For memory is not always correct; we sometimes think we remember various things, and it turns out that those things are not so; sometimes we are not sure, or simply do not know, whether we are remembering something or merely imagining it. This leads, as we saw in chapter 1, to the search for a "memory indicator," something that will mark off the genuine cases of memory from cases of mere imagination or of mistakenly thinking we remember. But the search proved unsuccessful; we saw that although we can tell—or rather, know without having to tell—whether we are trying to remember as opposed to deliberately making things up, there is no way of telling, from our remembering itself, whether we are remembering correctly or not. To establish that our memories are correct we have to get outside the remembering and compare what is remembered with the facts. But the trouble is it seems that the only way of getting at the facts is through memory.

Nor is this all. If we have no way of telling whether our memory is correct in any particular case, we have no way of telling whether it is ever correct. We are entitled to rely on something—be it a book, a newspaper, an expert, our senses, or our memories—only insofar as we can establish that it is normally an accurate guide to the facts of the matter. But if we can never tell when memory is correct and when it is not, we can never establish that it is a reliable guide to any- thing, and so we can never be entitled to rely on our memories. Unless we can show that mem- ory is often correct, we cannot show that it is reliable, and unless we can show that memory is reliable, we cannot be entitled to speak of memory-knowledge at all. Memory-beliefs, per- haps; certainly we all have them. But if I am to know something from memory, or because I re- member it, I have first to establish that my mem- ory is reliable, and to do that I need to establish that my memory is correct more often than not. This is the problem we have now to deal with, the problem of how memory-knowledge, of either sort, is possible.

One rather simple-minded approach to the problem would be to argue that memory is, by definition, infallible, insofar as we cannot be said to remember something unless it is so. But this purely verbal point does not solve the problem;

it merely shifts it. It may be that we cannot re-member a fact unless it is a fact, but the question remains of whether we are remembering when we think we are. The problem can be stated not in terms of remembering, but in terms of seeming to remember, or "ostensible remembering." Again, it can be argued that factual memory is, by defini-tion, a form of knowledge, so there can be no question but that we know what we factually re-member. But, once again, the problem is easily restated in other terms. The fact remains that we can think we are remembering when we are not, and the question remains of how we are to know whether and when cases of "ostensible" remem-bering are in fact cases of genuine remembering.

Another argument is that we cannot show that memory is unreliable without implicitly relying on memory. That is, we know that memory is not always correct only because we remember that it has let us down in the past, so the argument itself presupposes that memory is sometimes correct, viz., when it tells us we have gone wrong in the past: "There cannot be reasonable grounds for asserting or even for suspecting the falsity of any memory-judgement unless the infallibility of *some* memory-judgement is assumed" (Price, "Memory-Knowledge," pp. 23–24). Yet even if memory had never been shown to be incorrect, the problem of whether we can ever prove it correct would still remain; and, as Richard Brandt shows ("The Epistemological Status of Memory Beliefs," p. 81,

n. 3), we do not have to presuppose the correctness of one memory-judgment in order to show that some memory-judgments are false; if I now remember or think I remember that my memory has been mistaken in the past, then either my memory has been mistaken in the past or this present memory is mistaken. Either way, some memory is shown to be incorrect, without my having to assume the correctness of any particular piece of remembering.

Is there, then, any way in which we can check and verify our ostensible remembering? It may seem that there is. Suppose, for example, that I remember putting a knife in a drawer. I open the drawer, and there is the knife. Does that not confirm my memory—show that it did happen as I remember it? No, for the knife might be there without my having put it there. And this sort of difficulty will recur no matter what present evidence we produce in support of our memories of past events. "No one memory can be validated or invalidated without relying on other memories. . . . It is often supposed that we can validate or invalidate a memory-judgment by means of a present perception, for example by consulting documents or records. Again, it is supposed that we do it by appealing to the established laws of nature. . . . But in both cases we are using memory over again, because we are relying on inductive generalizations. . . . However great the probability of an inductive generalization may be, its probability is derived from *past* observations. We have only memory to assure us that those past observations existed, and what sort of observations they were" (Price, *Thinking and Experience*, pp. 78–79; see also Russell, *Inquiry into Meaning and Truth*, p. 157; and for a discussion of the point, Holland, "The Empiricist Theory of Memory," and Saunders, "Scepticism and Memory").

However, Harrod has suggested an ingenious way around this difficulty. He suggests that we can validate memory by present observation without appealing to memory, by verifying predictions based on what we remember: "The only procedure open to us appears to be to make predictions on the basis of the hypothesis that memory is informative, and test the hypothesis by their success and failure" ("Memory," p. 57). Thus, for example, I remember that lightning flashes have in the past instantly vanished in a way that hills and trees have not, so I predict that the lightning flash I now see will vanish in the same way, while the hills and trees I also see, will not. It happens as I predict, and memory is proved informative. However, as Harrod recognizes, the success of this prediction does not by itself establish that my memory of the past behavior of such things is correct. From the fact that hills and trees now remain while the lightning flash vanishes, it does not follow that such things have happened before, as I remember them happening. This is why Russell insists, "No memory proposition is, strictly speaking, verifiable, since nothing in the present or future makes any proposition about the past necessary" (*Inquiry into Meaning and Truth*, p. 154).

So if the present occurrence is to confirm my memory of such things having happened in the past, we will need some principle that connects present occurrences and past occurrences and, moreover, a principle that does not itself rely on memory. Harrod suggests the principle "that *if* certain things have been found to remain stable for some time, they are likely to continue so for a little longer" ("Memory," p. 61), which, he argues, is an a priori truth; experience, and experience alone, can tell us whether things are stable or not, but we do not need experience to know that things that remain stable for some time are likely to remain so a little longer. I do not myself find this suggestion particularly tempting, but, in any case, it is clear that the principle we need is not the one Harrod suggests, but rather its reverse—that if things happen in a certain way now, they are likely to have happened in the same way in the past. And I do not see how that principle can be shown true without appealing to memory.

Nonetheless, Harrod's discussion does suggest a possible way out of our difficulties. Clearly Harrod, Russell, and Price are all concentrating on our memory of the past, and it is just because the past is past that we have these problems. But although memory-knowledge and knowledge of the past are closely connected, it is a mistake to equate the two. There are ways of knowing what has happened besides remembering what has happened: from archaeological investigations; from library archives; from the simple realization that human monuments do not appear out of nowhere, so someone at some time must have constructed the objects we see around us. And on the other hand, as we have already seen, not all factual memory is knowledge of the past; the facts that we remember include facts about the present and the future, as when I remember that tomorrow is my wife's birthday. So let us for the moment ignore memory-knowledge of the past, with its special problems, and concentrate on factual memory, which relates to the present and the future. For if we can show that factual memory is reliable in these areas, perhaps we can then use it to confirm our memory of the past.

Something like this is suggested in Professor Furlong's modification of Harrod's argument, in his article also called "Memory." Furlong distinguishes between "retrospective" and "non-retrospective" memory, and shows that with the latter, at any rate, present experience can confirm the accuracy of our memories, can establish that what we remember is in fact the case. Thus, I remember that $2 + 2 = 4$; I work it out and, sure enough, 2 and 2 do come to 4. I remember that this switch works the heater; I turn it on and, sure enough, the heater goes on. Or to take Harrod's example construed as a case of non-retrospective memory, I remember that lightning flashes vanish and, sure enough, they do vanish. This may not prove that such things have happened in the past, as I remember them happening, but it does establish that the fact I claim to remember is a fact—lightning flashes do vanish instantly. Thus, time and time again, present experience confirms what we know from memory. How can there be any question but that factual memory, at any rate, is reliable?

Unfortunately, things are not quite so simple, for how do I know that factual memory has been shown to be accurate, time and time again? Surely I have to *remember* that it has, in which case factual memory is known to be reliable only by already relying on factual memory. I can use present experience to show that certain facts I seem to remember are indeed facts, that factual memory is accurate on particular occasions, but this will not get me very far toward showing that factual memory is reliable in general, unless I implicitly rely on my memory that this is what past experience has commonly shown. Furlong admits the difficulty in his later *Study in Memory* (pp. 64–66); indeed, he sees it as unavoidable. We consider something reliable because we *remember* that its information is generally accurate; it follows that "the very terms of our problem require an appeal to memory. We cannot validate memory without assuming memory." So, since "any validation whatever implies an appeal to memory," we have either to admit that any attempt to validate memory itself must inevitably beg the question, or to dismiss the problem as "obviously a pseudo-problem. There is no appeal beyond Caesar." But, either way, we can explain the layman's conviction that memory is trustworthy, for "memory . . . passes our common-sense test for reliability; its information is dependable; and that is the characteristic of a reliable witness."

It seems, then, that our problem of showing memory reliable turns out to be insoluble. We cannot rely on anything, not even memory itself, unless we already rely on memory, and, as J. T. Saunders puts it, "a circular justification is no justification at all" ("Scepticism and Memory," p. 485). Nevertheless, as Saunders goes on, "if this fact does not give us cause to rejoice, neither should its recognition provoke feelings of guilt or sorrow. It serves only to show that the reliability of ostensible memory is a fundamental assumption of the knowledge enterprise as we in fact pursue it. Such an enterprise must have its unprovable first principles (that is, principles which are unprovable within that enterprise). And surely it is interesting to note the logical role in which our memory beliefs are cast in virtue of one of the guiding principles of our cognitive life—the principle that our ostensible memories are, in general, to be relied upon."

We thus reach the conclusion often reached by Russell: ". . . that memory is in the main veridical is, in my opinion, one of the premisses of knowledge. . . . This is not logically necessary" (*Human Knowledge*, p. 288). I think, myself, that this is the correct conclusion, but it may well seem unsatisfactory in that we have not shown what we set out to show: that memory is reliable and so can provide us with, or constitute, knowledge. To say that the general reliability of memory is a contingent premise, an unprovable first principle, of human knowledge is still not to show that memory is reliable. But is this not to say, in effect, that human knowledge is based on an assumption, and one that might for all we know be mistaken? In that case, surely, we can do no more than assume that there is such a thing as memory-knowledge.

Certainly if that is the case, then this is a most unsatisfactory conclusion to reach. What we need, if we are to avoid it, is some justification for relying on memory as a contingent first premise of human knowledge, even though no non-circular proof of its reliability is possible. One suggestion, made by Richard Brandt, is that even if we cannot, in the last analysis, demonstrate that memory is reliable, this is nevertheless the simplest, indeed the only plausible, assumption to make when we come to explain the plain facts of the human situation. "Any satisfactory theory of nature obviously has to be based on, and explain, the unquestionable facts: the facts of present experience, and the fact of our memory beliefs. . . . When we begin looking about for a theory which will do what is wanted, we find that there is only one type of theory which comes near to success: a theory which postulates an historical sequence of events and human beings with a capacity to recall . . . and which hence explains memory beliefs as the precipitate of a process of interaction between human brain-minds and the world. In other words, the only acceptable theory is the one which asserts that a large proportion of our memory beliefs are veridical. No alternative to such a theory has been proposed; nor can we imagine what it would be like" ("The Epistemological Status of Memory Beliefs," pp. 92–93).

Now this would certainly be a reason for accepting that memory is reliable, were it not for the unfortunate fact that just such an alternative theory has been proposed, or at any rate suggested, as a logical possibility that has not yet been ruled out. This is the theory that there has actually been no past at all for us to remember or retain knowledge from, the theory that we have been created just as we are, complete with our existing but delusive memories. This theory seems farfetched, but unless we can rule it out, unless we can establish that there has been a past, as we all naturally think there has, we cannot accept Brandt's reason for allowing that memory is reliable. So in this way we come back to the problem we put on one side, the problem of our knowledge of the past.

This problem also comes up again in a rather different way, one that particularly concerns Von Leyden in his book *Remembering*. The hope was that we could confirm our memory of the past by first establishing the general reliability of factual memory. But even if we had been able to show that factual memory is generally reliable, by showing that present experience shows that most of the facts we seem to remember are facts, there is a further question that might be raised. For how, we might ask, are we to be sure that these facts are *remembered*? The claim to remember some fact involves the claim not only that it is a fact, but also that the knowledge was acquired in the past. But for all that present experience can show, it may be that something we claim to remember is not remembered at all but just happens, most conveniently, to come to mind without being information we acquired in the past. So if the claim to remember something, as opposed to the claim that what is said to be remembered is correct, is ever to be verified, we will need to have some knowledge of the past.

11

Our Knowledge of the Past

Not all memory-knowledge is knowledge of the past, and not all knowledge of the past is memory-knowledge. Nevertheless, we have just seen that the problem of memory-knowledge leads us to the problem of our knowledge of the past, and it might equally be argued that the problem of knowledge of the past leads to the problem of memory-knowledge, in that other ways of knowing what has happened themselves depend on and involve memory. Other sources can confirm and extend what we know from memory, but these other sources are themselves established and checked by reference to what we remember. (For an argument that statements about the past cannot be reduced to statements about present evidence, see Butler, "Other Dates," although curiously he thinks of this suggestion as opening the door to excessive skepticism rather than closing it; see also Ayer, "Statements about the Past.") Particularly when we turn to the question of how we know there has been a past at all, it seems we have to rely on memory. We know of a past because we know that time passes. And how do we know that time passes except by remembering what was before, and how it differs from what is now? There is, indeed, an even more basic question, the question of how we know what is meant by talk about "a past" in the first place, and it can be argued that our very concept of the past, like our knowledge of it, essentially involves memory. But there is not space to go into this aspect of the problem here (for references, see the bibliography). I am going to concentrate on the question of whether the past is knowable.

The difficulty is that the past has, by definition, passed. There is now no way in which we can recapture what has already happened or experience it again, except perhaps in memory if the Realist theory is correct. But this means there is now no way of establishing that what we remember, or think we remember, did happen. So, how can knowledge of the past be possible? "Remembering has to be a present occurrence in some way resembling, or related to, what is remembered. And it is difficult to find any ground, except a pragmatic one, for supposing that memory is not sheer delusion, if, as seems to be the case, there is not, apart from memory, any way of ascertaining that there really was a past occurrence having the required relation to our present remembering" (Russell, *Analysis of Mind,* p. 164). Indeed, if we cannot establish that things have happened as we remember them happening, can we establish that anything has ever happened at all? And so Russell is led to propose his famous hypothesis that, for all we know or can tell, there may have been no past at all, the whole world might have sprung into existence five minutes ago, complete with memories, records, geological traces, and so on.

Before we look at this hypothesis, however, there is the argument that it is a fundamental misconception to maintain that our knowledge of the past rests on memory. To make this point, J. O. Nelson draws a distinction between what he calls "memory-statements" and "past-tense ground-statements." A memory-statement incorporates the claim to remember something, so not all past-tense statements are memory-statements, and, says Nelson, the point of a memory-statement is that one is prepared to admit that one might be mistaken. We all know that memory is not infallible, so when we say "I remember such-and-such," we admit at least the possibility of error. Ground-statements, on the other hand, are such that we are not prepared to admit the possibility of error, so in such cases it would be incorrect to say "I remember. . . ." What we regard as ground-statements may differ from person to person and from situation to situation, but an example of an "absolute" past-tense ground-statement would be "I was alive last year." If such a ground-statement were overturned, "I could not retreat to the plea that I had a poor memory. Indeed, I would not know where to retreat to, unless to the plea of madness" ("The Validation of Memory," p. 38). Thus our knowledge of such things does not depend on memory, and we can therefore use this memory-independent knowledge, our own and other people's, to check and confirm and so establish the correctness of memory-statements about the past: "The independent confirmation of memory-statements consists in past-tense ground-statements" ("The Validation of Memory," p. 45).

It is true, of course, that it would be very odd to say "I remember that I was alive last year," and the explanation of this oddity may be as Nelson suggests—that we say "I remember" only where we are prepared to admit we could be wrong, whereas we are not prepared to admit we could be mistaken about something as basic as that. But whether or not my knowledge that I was alive last year could naturally be expressed in a memory-statement, this knowledge is, surely, memory-knowledge. It might be equally odd to suggest that this knowledge depends on personal memory, in that I know that I was alive last year only because I now remember being alive then. But it is, nevertheless, factual-memory knowledge, knowledge I have acquired from past experience and since retained. If I could not remember in this sense, i.e., could not retain information, then I would not know that I was alive last year. So, it is not true that my knowledge of past-tense ground-statements is independent of memory. The most we can claim is that it is independent of personal memory, and we have already seen (p. 99 above) that not all memory-knowledge rests on personal memory. But until we can establish the reliability of factual memory, unless we can show that such retained information is on the whole accurate, I cannot be entitled to rely on my conviction that I was alive last year—no matter how astonished I would be if that conviction proved mistaken. And, of course, Russell's suggestion is precisely that for all we know or can tell, that conviction might indeed be mistaken.

We return, therefore, to Russell's hypothesis. "It is not logically necessary to the existence of a memory-belief that the event remembered should have occurred, or even that the past should have existed at all. There is no logical impossibility in the hypothesis that the world sprang into being five minutes ago, exactly as it then was, with a population that "remembered" a wholly unreal past. There is no logically necessary connection between events at different times; therefore, nothing that is happening now or will ever happen in the future can disprove the hypothesis that the world began five minutes ago" (*Analysis of Mind*, pp. 159–60). No doubt, this suggestion seems excessively fanciful—though something very like it seems to have been held by the Fundamentalist biologist Philip Gosse, who argued that God had created the world in 4004 B.C., complete with fossils, rock strata, etc., which he placed there in order to test our faith in his revealed word. But as Russell goes on, "I am not suggesting that the non-existence of the past should be entertained as a serious hypothesis. Like all sceptical hypotheses, it is logically tenable, but uninteresting."

The question is, then, whether Russell's hypothesis is the genuine, though uninteresting(!), possibility he says it is, for it is this logical possibility that affects our claim to have knowledge of the past and, as we saw, our right to rely on memory. The pity of it is that Russell seems to be right. Not that the hypothesis seems correct; on the contrary, a suggestion as strange as this one would need a lot of swallowing, and Russell has given us not the slightest reason for swallowing it. Indeed, he could not do so; the hypothesis is as impossible to prove correct as it is to prove incorrect, and for the same reasons. But on the face of it, the hypothesis does seem to be a logical possibility. Recently, however, there have been ingenious attempts to show that it is not. Both Norman Malcolm ("Three Lectures on Memory," pp. 187 ff.) and Sydney Shoemaker (*Self-Knowledge and Self-Identity*, pp. 228 ff., and "Memory," p. 273) argue that it is not a contingent fact that memory-beliefs and memory-claims are generally true, and so not a logical possibility that they are one and all false. This means not only that Russell's hypothesis is not a logical possibility, after all, but also that it is a necessary, conceptual fact that memory is, in general, reliable. Such an argument would solve all our problems.

The argument, as stated by Shoemaker, is that Russell's hypothesis "rests on the idea that it can only be contingently true, if it is true at all, that memory beliefs are for the most part true. If this were so, we ought to be able to imagine finding a people whose memories were seldom or never correct. But supposing that there could be such a people, how could we identify any of their utterances as memory claims (as we would have to be able to do in order to find that their memory claims are mostly false)? We would not be satisfied that one of our own children had learned the correct use of the word "remember" and of the expressions that indicate a past tense unless the sincere statements he made by the use of these expressions were normally true—just as we would not allow that someone knew the meaning of the word "blue" if he typically applied it to such things as grass and trees. In this case, as in many others, using an expression correctly necessarily goes together with using it to make statements that are (for the most part) true. . . . If the language of a people were translated in a certain way and it turned out that the utterances translated as memory claims nearly always had to be regarded as false, this would surely be conclusive grounds for saying that these utterances were not memory claims at all and that the language had been mistranslated" ("Memory," p. 273). Thus, if there are to be memory claims at all, or, Malcolm would add, past-tense statements generally, most of them will have to be true; it is not possible that there could be memory claims or past-tense statements that are generally false.

It seems to me that this argument cannot be quite right (for a discussion, see J. W. Cornman, "Malcolm's Mistaken Memory" and "More on Mistaken Memory"; and A. Naylor, "On 'Remembering' an Unreal Past"). It would mean, for example, that if someone were hypnotized so that he forgot everything he knew about the past, and instead seemed to remember things that never happened, we would have to say not that he was misremembering, but that he had lost his understanding of the past tense. Similarly, if the universe were to be annihilated or altered in such a way that all our future-tense statements turned out to be false, it would follow, according to a similar argument, that we had not understood the correct use of future-tense statements. Of course, whether or not past- or future-tense statements are true, depends on what has happened or will happen, but it can hardly be that our present understanding of such statements is determined by what has happened or will happen.

The argument turns on the claim that "using an expression correctly necessarily goes together with using it to make statements that are (for the most part) true," or as Malcolm puts it (p. 196), "Knowing how to use the past tense cannot be completely separated from making many true statements with it." But suppose that someone believes in the existence of goblins and gnomes and is continually telling us about what they do to each other, to him, and to us. All these assertions about goblins and gnomes are false, but what he says may still show that he understands the terms he is using, and in that sense knows how to use them correctly. Similarly, statements made by superstitious tribes about spirits and demons are generally false, without our concluding that we must therefore have mistranslated them. And would Shoemaker argue, as he argues about memory-claims, that "if the language of a people were translated in a certain way and it turned out that the utterances translated as claims about spirits and demons nearly always had to be regarded as false, this would surely be conclusive grounds for saying that these utterances were not claims about spirits and demons at all and that the language had been mistranslated"?

Thus knowing how to use an expression does not necessarily go together with using it to make true statements; a person could use an expression correctly, in the sense of using it with its correct meaning, and yet seldom, if ever, say anything true with it. Habitual mistakes could be due to a mistake of terminology, as in Shoemaker's example of the man who applies "blue" to such things as grass and trees, but they might equally be due to some deep-rooted mistake of fact, as with the man who believes that his household accidents are the work of goblins and gnomes. What shows that the man misunderstands the word "blue," however, is not that what he says is false, but that what he means by that expression is not what the expression is correctly used to mean. Of course, whether or not we correctly understand the expressions we use is established by what we say with them, but what counts is not whether what is said is true, but what it is that we mean to assert by means of them. We discover whether a man understands an expression by discovering what he thinks he is saying when he uses that expression and what he thinks would make it true, not by discovering whether what he says is true. If someone says there is a goblin in his chimney, meaning to assert that his chimney contains a small malevolent being with a pointed head and supernatural powers, then his saying what he does demonstrates that he understands the word "goblin" and is here using it correctly, even though what he says is false.

So even if all our memory claims and past-tense statements were false, it would not follow that we were misusing the word "remember" or misunderstanding the past tense. So long as we can establish that we use the past tense to talk about things that, as we believe, did happen—and not, for example, about events we ascribe to our dreams—then we can establish that we are using the past tense correctly, even if all our past-tense statements are in fact false. Russell's hypothesis remains a logical possibility.

Malcolm has two further arguments against Russell's suggestion. The first is that Russell supposes that, although the past is totally unreal, nevertheless memories and records and so on agree, as they do, about what is believed to have happened. "But if there was this kind of agreement, then the apparent memories would be verified as true. This is what the verification of apparent memories *means*. . . . And if the apparent memories were verified, it would not be intelligible to hold that, nevertheless, the past they describe may not have existed. . . . The supposed unreal past has turned out to be real" (pp. 198–99). I believe that this argument plays upon an ambiguity in the word "verify." Verification can mean establishing that something is so, which we cannot do unless it is so. But it can also mean checking whether it is so, which we can do even if it is not so. Thus, I might verify a date by looking it up in a book, and yet still get it wrong because the book is wrong, too. Malcolm says that if we check a memory against other people's memories and against the records and so on, then we have done all we can to verify it. The population of Russell's hypothesized world can do all this, and if they do, says Malcolm, they have then verified their apparent memories. And if they have verified those memories, the memories must be correct, so Russell's hypothesis destroys itself. But clearly Malcolm has shifted, from verification in the sense of checking the memories, to verification in the sense of establishing that they are correct. Russell's population can do everything possible to verify their memories in the sense of checking them, but they have still failed to verify those memories in the sense of establishing that they are correct, for as Russell describes it, those memories are mistaken all along. When Malcolm says, ". . . if there was this kind of agreement, then the apparent memories would be verified as true," this means only that the checking would have confirmed the memories, not that the checking would have shown them to be true. *Ex hypothesi*, they are false.

Malcolm's final objection is that Russell's hypothesis "is incompatible with the very concept of *evidence*. . . . To accept this 'hypothesis' as true would mean the destruction of *all* our thinking" ("Three Lectures on Memory," p. 201). Others have made similar points. It is clear, for a start, that the hypothesis can be neither proved nor disproved, and "with no conceivable way of establishing its truth or falsehood, one is inclined to balk at admitting it as a genuine hypothesis at all" (Butler, "Other Dates," p. 18). In this, perhaps, it is like all specifically philosophical hypotheses; being philosophical, they are not hypotheses open to eventual confirmation or refutation. But it is not just that the hypothesis cannot be proved or disproved; we cannot even produce evidence either way, since any possible evidence would itself fall within the scope of the hypothesis. Some philosophers (e.g., Butler, "Other Dates," p. 18; F. Waismann, *Principles of Linguistic Philosophy*, pp. 20–21) conclude from this that the hypothesis becomes meaningless. For if it were correct, there would be no criteria for distinguishing genuine memory from mere imagination, and the suggestion that nothing is remembered, everything is imagined, would turn out to be meaningless. It is often hard to know what precisely philosophers mean when they talk about criteria, but this argument seems to me a disguised application of the verification theory of meaning, the theory that a statement has meaning only to the extent that it is capable of verification. That is, the argument seems to be that, on Russell's hypothesis, there is no way of telling whether we are remembering or imagining. That of course is so; it is the very point of the hypothesis. But to insist that talk about memory and imagination makes sense only if we can verify claims about what is remembered or imagined, is to adopt a widely rejected theory of meaning. If, on the other hand, the argument is that, on Russell's hypothesis, there is no way of making a conceptual distinction between memory and imagination, the argument is mistaken. For the meanings and truth conditions of memory and imagination statements remain the same, whether Russell's hypothesis is correct or not.

However, the peculiarity of Russell's hypothesis does not stop at the fact that evidence for or against it is impossible. The crucial oddity is that the hypothesis itself is formulated in such a way as to make such evidence logically impossible. One might say that, although the hypothesis does not refute itself, as self-contradictions do, it nevertheless disqualifies itself as a hypothesis, by itself ruling out any possibility of there being any evidence about it. Thus Marcus Singer points out that the question whether the world came into existence five minutes ago, complete as it then was, is so framed that any answer to it must beg the question; and a question that makes it logically impossible for us to give an answer must be a senseless question. "No instances of memory, no amount of remains, records or testimony, and no number of general laws that seem relevant to a question about the past, and ordinarily are relevant, would be relevant in this case. . . . It is impossible to conceive of anything that might possibly serve as evidence for an answer that would not itself come within the terms of the question. . . . This is why any proposed answer . . . would be question-begging, and this is why it is logically impossible for the question to be answered. It is not that one could not formulate an answer which in its form would be an answer to the question; it is rather that one could not possibly, given the structure of the question, supply any evidence that this proposition is true." ("Meaning, Memory and the Moment of Creation," p. 190).

I think we can agree with Singer that a question that cannot, logically cannot, be answered must be senseless as a question, but, as Singer concedes, it does not follow that what is said in the question is, as such, meaningless. Russell's hypothesis is formulated so as to destroy the very possibility of our having evidence either way, but this does not in itself render the hypothesis incoherent or inconceivable. However, Malcolm's point cuts much deeper than any of this; it is not just that the hypothesis rules out the possibility of evidence for or against that hypothesis, but that it destroys any possibility of our having evidence about anything. "Consider what would be implied by our 'believing' that the earth and mankind had just come into existence. If one of us were to 'believe' this, he would have to renounce not only his previous conception of his own identity, but his entire store of common knowledge. . . . If he thought out the consequences of this hypothesis, he would realise that it is not anything he could rationally believe, because 'believing' it would mean that he no longer understood anything at all" ("Three Lectures on Memory," pp. 200–1). If there has been no past then we have no past history, and if we have no past history we have never acquired any information nor any reason for believing anything, not even about the present. Without a past, I could not have learned what tables are, and so could have no reason for thinking this to be a table I am writing on. And since, if Russell's hypothesis were correct, we could have no reason for regarding anything as correct, it follows that we would then have no reason for regarding the hypothesis itself as correct. It is, in short, not something that can rationally be believed, for to believe it would mean we had no reason for believing it.

Perhaps it does not follow from this that a rational man must believe the hypothesis false. There is always the possibility of remaining agnostic about this curious possibility, and as long as we cannot actually prove it false, that might seem to be the rational course. But this is to forget the scope of Malcolm's argument; if the hypothesis were correct, we would have no reason for believing anything. We have, therefore, the alternative of rejecting the hypothesis or of believing nothing. It seems clear which of the two a rational man must choose if he is to be a rational man at all. This, in the end, is the importance of C. I. Lewis' point: "If we adopt the Cartesian method of doubting everything which admits of doubt, we must stop short of doubting this. Because to doubt our sense of past experience as founded in actuality, would be to lose any criterion by which either the doubt itself or what is doubted could be corroborated; and to erase altogether the distinction between empirical fact and fantasy. In that sense, we have no rational alternative but to presume that everything sensed as past is just a little more probable than that which is incompatible with what is remembered and that with respect to which memory is blank" (*Analysis of Knowledge and Valuation*, p. 358).

The conclusion is, then, that we have no rational alternative but to regard Russell's hypothesis as false. This is not to establish that it is false. The only way we could do that, given the nature of the hypothesis, is by showing it to be somehow incoherent, and I do not see that this has been shown. Indeed, it seems to me that, as a matter of common sense, the possibility is always a possibility, though no more; it is logically possible, but not, as Russell says, logically tenable. It may seem unsatisfactory to conclude that we have reasons for rejecting the hypothesis, but reasons that are not such as to prove it false. But this is not quite to say, as Russell does, that our only ground for supposing that memory is not sheer delusion is a pragmatic one, at least not if the "pragmatic ground" is simply that it is convenient and useful. The point is stronger than that; it is that rationality itself requires that we accept our evidence for the past as evidence for the past, even though we cannot, in the last analysis, prove that there has been the past that this evidence points to. So it is not just a matter of what proves convenient; it is a matter of what presuppositions or assumptions we have to make if knowledge is to become possible at all. And this same conclusion can now be applied to memory generally.

12

The Indispensability of Memory-Knowledge

We have seen that, if we are to be rational, if we are to have any reason for believing anything, we cannot believe that the world has just sprung into existence. We have also seen that we cannot establish the general reliability of memory without already relying on memory. But can we perhaps justify our reliance on our memory-beliefs in something the way we justify our belief that there has been a past? For memory-knowledge is an indispensable element in human knowledge; most of the things we know we know because we remember them, and the progress of knowledge, or even the day-to-day conduct of our lives, would be quite impossible without the ability to remember. Indeed without memory we could not even have knowledge of our present environments; I could not know that this is a table I am now writing on if I could not remember what tables are. So without memory one could know nothing at all, and there would be no such thing as human knowledge.

Norman Malcolm draws an even stronger conclusion—that without memory we could scarcely be human. "A being without factual memory would not have the ability to remember that he was about to do so-and-so or that he had been doing such-and-such. He would not remember where he had put anything, where he was, or when he was to do a certain thing. A being without factual memory would have no mental powers to speak of, and he would not really be a man even if he had the human form" ("Three Lectures on Memory," p. 212). He later makes a similar point about personal memory: "Could creatures who never remembered anything they perceived or experienced, have anything like human powers? Surely not. For one thing, these creatures would not be able to *recognize* any particular person or object. This alone would imply that they could not have many of the concepts that human beings have, and could not do many of the things that human beings do" (p. 221). And so Malcolm concludes, as against Russell's claim that what he called "true memory" is the "sort of occurrence that constitutes the essence of memory" (*Analysis of Mind*, p. 167), that "both factual and personal memory are essential to mankind. They are so thoroughly entwined with one another that it would be impossible to say which is *more* essential" (p. 221).

We see, then, that we must be prepared to rely on what we remember or seem to remember if there is to be human knowledge at all or, indeed, if we are to be human in the first place. This has two important consequences. The first is that, when earlier (p. 112 above) we were worried by the fact that the reliability of memory has to be accepted, without proof, as a contingent premise or first principle of human knowledge, we were quite wrong to be worried by it, since it is not something that could possibly be otherwise. Although it may be a contingent fact that ostensible memory is generally reliable, it is a necessary logical truth that we cannot prove that fact. For any such proof must rest on premises known to be true, and if all knowledge presupposes memory, it follows that we cannot prove anything about memory or about anything else without already relying on memory. This is not an unfortunate situation that we might wish were otherwise; we cannot hope to establish the reliability of memory by a non-circular argument any more than we can hope to draw a round square. If someone is worried by the fact that we cannot establish the reliability of memory except by taking it for granted, then, as Ayer says about the skeptic who doubts or denies our knowledge of the past in particular, "our only recourse is to point out . . . that the proof he requires of us is one that he makes it logically impossible for us to give. It is, therefore, not surprising that we cannot furnish it: it is no discredit to the proofs that we do rely on, that they do not imply that we can achieve the impossible; it would be a discredit to them, rather, if they did" (*Problem of Knowledge*, p. 164).

The second point is that we now have the justification of our reliance on memory for which we were looking. We saw that the general reliability of memory can be described as a first principle of human knowledge, but since this "first principle" is contingent, and yet, in the last analysis, unprovable, it looked as though human knowledge must therefore be built on an unjustified, indeed an unjustifiable, assumption. But we can now see that the assumption is reasonable, at least in that it has to be made if knowledge is ever to be possible at all.

This amounts, I think, to a "transcendental argument" for the reliability of memory. A transcendental argument is one that shows that a certain principle, though logically contingent in itself, has nevertheless to be accepted as true if a certain form of inquiry or a certain sphere of discourse is to be possible. A valid transcendental argument faces us with a choice of either accepting the principle in question, or of giving up the particular inquiry or subject matter. This, it seems, is the position we are in with regard to our reliance on memory; we have either to accept this reliance as legitimate, or give up all claim to knowledge of the past or acquired in the past or in any way based on such knowledge. What we cannot do is put our reliance on memory in question and then demonstrate the reliability of ostensible remembering. This is to attempt the impossible; memory-knowledge, and with it, knowledge generally, is possible only insofar as we are prepared to accept memory as reliable.

Perhaps it is worth repeating that none of this shows that it is a necessary or logical truth that memory is reliable, or that our reliance on memory cannot legitimately be questioned at all. The point is rather that it can, but only at a price, the price of giving up all claims to our "store of common knowledge," as Malcolm calls it. Sydney Shoemaker argues against this, that we have to accept it as a necessary truth that confident memory beliefs, and similarly confident perceptual beliefs, are generally true, if we are ever to know anything on the basis of memory or perception. For, he argues, "if it is a contingent fact, which could be otherwise, that my confident perceptual and memory beliefs are generally true, and if I cannot establish this fact on the basis of observation and memory" (as I cannot do without begging the question) "then surely there is *no* way in which I could establish it" (*Self-Knowledge and Self-Identity*, p. 235). But it does not follow from this argument, that we have to take the reliability of memory to be a necessary truth; knowledge depends on its being a fact that memory is reliable, not on its being a necessary or logical fact. I suspect that Shoemaker has in mind the traditional, and I believe oversimple, distinction between contingent truths, which are established by reference to such things as perception and memory, and logical truths, which do not need to be established in this way. So, since perception and memory cannot be used to establish that perception and memory themselves are reliable, it must, he thinks, be a logical truth that they are reliable, if it is to be true at all. But we need not go to this extreme. A transcendental argument is, precisely, a way of showing that we have to accept something as true even though it is neither a necessary truth nor one that can be established by experience.

One main function of such arguments is to show how certain presuppositions, if you like, are essential to various modes of human thought. This must be the conclusion of our discussion of memory-knowledge: there is such a thing as memory-knowledge, memory has to be accepted as reliable, because without it there would be no knowledge at all, in particular no knowledge of the past. One cannot question the possibility of memory-knowledge without shaking the entire structure of human knowledge to its foundations.

And that, of course, is precisely what the philosophical skeptic means to do.

Bibliography

This is a list of all works cited in the text, together with all writings on memory published since 1945 that I have been able to trace. Works marked with an asterisk are especially recommended.

MEMORY

S. Alexander, *Space, Time and Deity,* Dover and Macmillan, 1920, chap. 4.

Aristotle, "On Memory and Reminiscence," in R. McKeon, ed., *The Basic Works of Aristotle,* Random House, 1941.

St. Augustine, *Confessions,* Bk. X, secs. 8–19.

* A. J. Ayer, *The Problem of Knowledge,* Penguin Books, 1956, chap. 4 (see reviews by P. F. Strawson, *Philosophy,* 1957, and H. H. Price, *Mind,* 1958).

B. S. Benjamin, "Remembering," *Mind,* 1956.

H. Bergson, *Matter and Memory,* Humanities and Allen and Unwin, 1912, chap. 5.

R. Brandt, "The Epistemological Status of Memory Beliefs," *Philosophical Review,* 1955.

C. D. Broad, *Mind and Its Place in Nature,* Humanities and Kegan Paul, 1925, chap. 5.

Bibliography

R. J. Butler, "Other Dates," *Mind*, 1959.

J. W. Cornman, "Malcolm's Mistaken Memory," *Analysis*, 1964–65.

J. W. Cornman, "More on Mistaken Memory," *Analysis*, 1966–67.

W. Earle, "Memory," *Review of Metaphysics*, 1956–57.

E. J. Furlong, "Memory," *Mind*, 1948.

E. J. Furlong, *A Study in Memory*, Humanities and Nelson, 1951 (see review by H. H. Price, *Philosophical Quarterly*, 1957).

E. J. Furlong, "Memory and the Argument from Illusion," *Proceedings of the Aristotelian Society*, 1953–54.

E. J. Furlong, "The Empiricist Theory of Memory," *Mind*, 1956.

R. F. Harrod, "Memory," *Mind*, 1942.

R. F. Harrod, *Foundations of Inductive Logic*, Macmillan, 1956, chap. 8.

J. W. Harvey, "Knowledge of the Past," *Proceedings of the Aristotelian Society*, 1940–41.

* R. F. Holland, "The Empiricist Theory of Memory," *Mind*, 1954 (see also Furlong, "The Empiricist Theory of Memory"; Saunders, "Scepticism and Memory").

D. Hume, *Treatise of Human Nature*, Bk. I, pt. I, sec. 3; Bk. I, pt. III, sec. 5.

J. Laird, *Study in Realism*, Cambridge, 1920, chap. 3.

J. Laird, *Knowledge, Belief and Opinion*, The Century Co., 1930, chap. 13.

C. Landesman, "Philosophical Problems of Memory," *Journal of Philosophy*, 1962.

C. I. Lewis, *An Analysis of Knowledge and Valuation*, Open Court, 1946, chap. 11, secs. 6, 10, 11.

D. Locke, "Memory, Memories and Me," in *Knowledge and Necessity,* Macmillan, 1970.

J. Locke, *Essay Concerning Human Understanding,* Bk. II, chap. 10.

* N. Malcolm, "Three Lectures on Memory," *Knowledge and Certainty,* Prentice-Hall, 1963 (see also Cornman, "Malcolm's Mistaken Memory"; Naylor, "On 'Remembering' an Unreal Past"; Cornman, "More on Mistaken Memory"; Munsat, "A Note on Factual Memory"; Munsat, "Does All Memory Imply Factual Memory?").

* C. Martin and M. Deutscher, "Remembering," *Philosophical Review,* 1966 (see also Squires, "Memory Unchained").

G. E. Moore, *Some Main Problems of Philosophy,* Collier and Allen and Unwin, 1953, pp. 237–47.

S. Munsat, "A Note on Factual Memory," *Philosophical Studies,* 1965.

S. Munsat, "Does All Memory Imply Factual Memory?" *Analysis Supplement,* 1965.

S. Munsat, *The Concept of Memory,* Random House, 1966.

A. Naylor, "On 'Remembering' an Unreal Past," *Analysis,* 1965–66.

J. O. Nelson, "The Validation of Memory and Our Conception of a Past," *Philosophical Review,* 1963.

H. H. Price, "Memory-Knowledge," *Proceedings of the Aristotelian Society, Supplementary Volume,* 1936.

H. H. Price, *Thinking and Experience,* Hutchinson, 1953.

Bibliography

* T. Reid, *Essays on the Intellectual Powers of Man*, W. Hamilton, ed., James Thin, 1895, essay 3.

B. Russell, *The Analysis of Mind*, Humanities and Allen and Unwin, 1921, chap. 9.

B. Russell, *Inquiry into Meaning and Truth*, Humanities and Allen and Unwin, 1940, pp. 154–61.

B. Russell, *Human Knowledge: Its Scope and Limits*, Simon and Schuster, Allen and Unwin, 1948.

B. Russell, *Problems of Philosophy*, Home University Library, Oxford University Press, 1912.

G. Ryle, *The Concept of Mind*, Barnes and Noble, Hutchinson, 1949, chap. 8, sec. 7.

* J. T. Saunders, "Scepticism and Memory," *Philosophical Review*, 1963.

S. Shoemaker, *Self-Knowledge and Self-Identity*, Cornell, 1963.

* S. Shoemaker, "Memory," in *The Encyclopedia of Philosophy*, Macmillan and Free Press, 1967.

M. G. Singer, "Meaning, Memory and the Moment of Creation," *Proceedings of the Aristotelian Society*, 1962–63.

B. Smith, *Memory*, Humanities and Allen and Unwin, 1966.

J. R. Squires, "Memory Unchained," *Philosophical Review*, 1969.

G. H. Stout, *Mind and Matter*, Cambridge, 1931, Bk. III, chap. 5.

G. H. Stout, "In What Way Is Memory-Knowledge Immediate?" *Studies in Philosophy and Psychology*, Macmillan, 1930.

R. Taylor, "The 'Justification' of Memories and the Analogy of Vision," *Philosophical Review*, 1956.

J. O. Urmson, "Memory and Imagination," *Mind*, 1967.

W. von Leyden, *Remembering: A Philosophical Problem,* Duckworth, 1961.

F. Waismann, *The Principles of Linguistic Philosophy,* St. Martins and Macmillan, 1965, chap. II, sec. 1.

A. D. Woozley, *Theory of Knowledge,* Hutchinson, 1949; Barnes and Noble, 1966, chaps. 2, 3.

E. M. Zemach, "A Definition of Memory," *Mind,* 1968.

OUR CONCEPT OF THE PAST

G. E. M. Anscombe, "The Reality of the Past," *Philosophical Analysis,* ed. M. Black, Cornell University Press, 1950.

A. J. Ayer, "Statements About the Past," *Philosophical Essays,* St. Martins and Macmillan, 1954.

A. J. Ayer, *The Problem of Knowledge,* Penguin Books, 1956, chap. 4, secs. iv, v.

E. J. Bond, "The Concept of the Past," *Mind,* 1963.

M. Dummett, "The Reality of the Past," *Proceedings of the Aristotelian Society,* 1968–69.

MENTAL IMAGERY

A. Flew, "Facts and Imagination," *Mind,* 1956.

G. B. Mathews, "Mental Copies," *Philosophical Review,* 1969.

G. Ryle, *The Concept of Mind,* Barnes and Noble and Hutchinson, 1949, chap. 8.

J. M. Shorter, "Imagination," *Mind,* 1952.

J. R. Squires, "Visualizing," *Mind,* 1968.

Index

In memory, we seem to be acquainted with the past. But how can we be acquainted with what no longer exists? And how can we be sure that things have happened as we remember them?

Don Locke is here concerned with these and other philosophical problems of memory, seeking to determine if memory can be shown to be reliable, and so to provide a source or a form of knowledge. He gives a clear, concise and critical account of discussion from Aristotle to the present day. Special attention is given to contemporary discussion and controversy, though traditional considerations receive their due weight.

This is a lucid and indispensable guide to the subject.

For a biographical note on the author, please see the back flap

Don Locke lectures in Philosophy at the University of Warwick. His publications include *Perception and Our Knowledge of the External World* (1967) and *Myself and Others* (1968).

Index